A QUICK COURSE IN

WORDPERFECT

For Windows

KAYE FOX

POLLY URBAN

MARILEE RICHINS

PUBLISHED BY
Online Press Incorporated
14320 NE 21st Street, Suite 18
Bellevue, WA 98007
(800) 854-3344

Publisher's Cataloging in Publication
(prepared by Quality Books Inc.)

Fox, Kaye, 1932–
    A Quick Course in WordPerfect for Windows / Kaye Fox, Polly Urban, Marilee Richins.
    --

    p. cm.
    Includes index.
    ISBN 1-879399-06-7

    1. WordPerfect (Computer program) 2. Word processing.   I.
Urban, Polly.   II. Richins, Marilee.   III. Title.

    Z52.5.F6 1991   652'.5'536
                                                QBI91-1724
                                                        91-67583
                                                            CIP

Printed and bound in the United States of America

1 2 3 4 5 6 7 8 9 W P F W 3 2 1 0

Distributed to bookstores by Publishers Group West, (800) 788-3123

Bitstream® is a registered trademark of Bitstream Inc. Quattro® and Quattro Pro® are registered trademarks of Borland International, Inc. Hewlett-Packard® and LaserJet® are registered trademarks of Hewlett-Packard Company. IBM® is a registered trademark of International Business Machines Corporation. SigmaPlot™is a trademark of Jandel Scientific. Lotus® and 1-2-3® are registered trademarks of Lotus Development Corporation. Windows™ is a trademark of Microsoft Corporation. PlanPerfect® and WordPerfect® are registered trademarks of WordPerfect Corporation. Paintbrush® is a registered trademark of ZSoft Corporation. All other products mentioned in this book are trademarks of their respective owners.

All product and company names used in the example notes, memos, letters, and reports in this book are fictitious and do not represent any existing product or company. Any resemblance to an actual product or company name is coincidental and unintentional.

Contents

Introduction

People learn in different ways. And that's why there are so many different books about WordPerfect for Windows to choose from. How do you know which book is right for you? A lot depends on your style of learning.

Some people want a 900-page book that describes bit by bit every last detail of the program. Others are satisfied with a quick reference guide that they can pick up occasionally when they get stumped about how to implement a particular command or feature. In Quick Course books, we take another approach. We train you to use WordPerfect for Windows to create professional documents that you can actually use in your business; and at the same time we teach the most-often used features of the program.

To teach WordPerfect for Windows, we begin with a brief memo. We then go on to show you step by step how to create professional-looking business letters, letterheads, and reports that include tables and charts. Along the way, we demonstrate how to take advantage of WordPerfect for Windows' intuitive point-and-click interface by using the new Button Bar, the time-saving Ruler, and the many commands now accessible through menus. We teach you how, with a few clicks of the mouse, you can create and format great-looking documents, and we show how to dress up your documents using the graphics included with the WordPerfect program, as well as artwork created in other programs. In addition, we help you organize files using File Manager and put File Manager's powerful search capabilities to work finding your files. Finally, we explore ways to streamline office mailings by using WordPerfect for Windows' Merge feature to print form documents and envelopes.

As in all Quick Course books, we supplement the instructions and discussions in this book with handy tips and other useful items that might not be critical to the topic at hand but that you might find interesting or helpful as you learn the program. We begin each chapter by showing the document we will help you create and, as a memory jogger, we indicate the pages on which you can find important information about specific features that you might want to look up later. In addition, we place arrows in the margins at various locations throughout the chapter to point out procedures you might find yourself using repeatedly, making them easy to spot as you thumb through the book.

For the most part, we use Windows conventions when describing procedures. We assume you are using a mouse, but give the keyboard equivalents of commands for those times when keeping your hands on the keys is more efficient than reaching for the mouse. We indicate any text you need to type in italics and use standard IBM names for the keys, such as Del for the delete key and Ins for the insert key.

That said, let's move on to memos and start taking advantage of the many exciting features of this extraordinarily popular software program.

1

First Things First

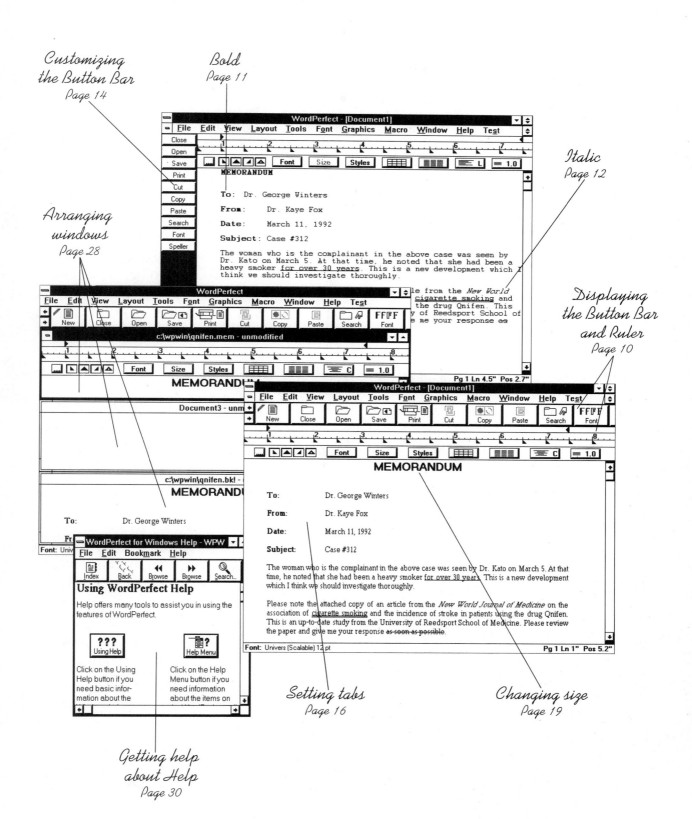

Customizing the Button Bar
Page 14

Bold
Page 11

Italic
Page 12

Arranging windows
Page 28

Displaying the Button Bar and Ruler
Page 10

Setting tabs
Page 16

Changing size
Page 19

Getting help about Help
Page 30

Y ou're probably sitting at your computer with the C> prompt on your screen. More than likely, you have letters and reports to write, and you're anxious to get started with WordPerfect for Windows. But first we need to cover some basics, such as how to enter text, get around WordPerfect's Editing screen, select parts of a document, give instructions, save and retrieve documents, and—very important—get help when you need it. Along the way, we review some Windows techniques, but we assume that you have already used Windows enough to be familiar with basic Windows operations. (If you are new to Windows as well as new to WordPerfect for Windows, we suggest you take a look at *A Quick Course in Windows*, another book in the Quick Course series, which will bring you quickly up to speed.) After you learn a few fundamentals, you'll easily be able to create the documents we cover in the rest of the book.

Getting Started

We assume that you've already installed both Windows and WordPerfect for Windows on your computer, and that you're ready to go. (We don't give detailed instructions for installing the program because the process is so easy. Insert the Install disk in your A drive, type *a:install*, and press Enter. WordPerfect will then guide you through the fast and efficient installation process.)

We also assume that you're using a mouse. Although it is possible to work with WordPerfect for Windows using only the keyboard, the Windows environment is tailor-made for point-and-click mouse techniques, and using a mouse with WordPerfect for Windows is both intuitive and efficient.

Starting WordPerfect for Windows

The simplest way to start WordPerfect for Windows is from the Windows Program Manager. Follow these steps:

1. Type *win* at the C> prompt, and press Enter.
2. If necessary, double-click the WordPerfect icon to open the WordPerfect group window.
3. In the group window, double-click the WP icon to start the program. WordPerfect's copyright screen makes a brief appearance, and a few seconds later, you see this Editing screen:

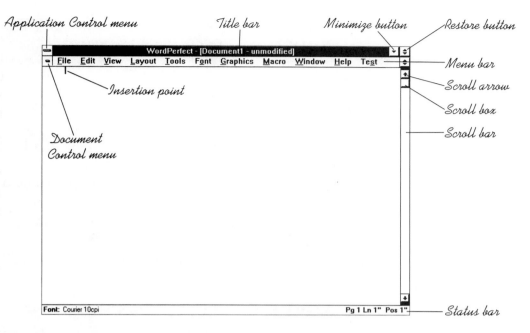

Not much to it, is there? At the top, the title bar tells you that you are looking at Document1 and that you have not yet modified the document. As soon as you type something or choose a command, *unmodified* will disappear, letting you know that the document has changed since you last saved it. At the bottom, the status bar gives you useful information about the document in areas called *fields*. For example, on the right the Pg field tells you which page you are on (in this case, page 1), and the Ln and Pos fields give your position, in inches, from the top and left margin of the page.

We'll discuss the other labeled elements as we use them in this chapter. For now, let's get down to business.

Entering Text

So that you have something to work with as we show you how to move around, give instructions, and save files, let's create our first document, a memo. You can follow along with our example or type a memo of your own.

1. Press the Caps Lock key to turn on capitalization.

2. Type *memorandum* as the memo title. As you type, the insertion point (or cursor) leads the way, showing you where the next character you type will be inserted.

Capital letters

Memo headings →

3. To turn off capitalization, press the Caps Lock key again, and then press Enter to move to the next line.

4. Press Enter two more times to add two blank lines beneath the memo title.

5. Type *To:*, press the Tab key, and type *Dr. George Winters*.

6. Press Enter twice to end the line and add a blank line below it.

7. Type *From:*, press the Tab key, type *Dr. Kaye Fox*, and then press Enter twice.

8. Type *Date:*, press the Tab key, type today's date, and then press Enter twice.

9. Type *Subject:*, press Tab, type *Case #312*, and then press Enter twice. Here's the result so far:

Some basics

In case you're new to computers, you hold down the Shift key while pressing other keys to enter individual capital (uppercase) letters, and you press the Backspace key to erase mistakes. ♦

The Pos field

Turning on Caps Lock changes the appearance of the Pos field in the status bar at the bottom of the screen. When you press Caps Lock, *Pos* becomes *POS*. Turning off the feature returns the Pos field to normal. ♦

Starting over

If you make a mistake while creating the memo (or any other document in this book) and want to start over with a clear screen, simply choose the Close command from the File menu, and then click No when WordPerfect asks whether you want to save the changes. (See page 9 if you need help choosing commands.) ♦

10. Now type the following message (or your own message), pressing Enter twice between paragraphs:

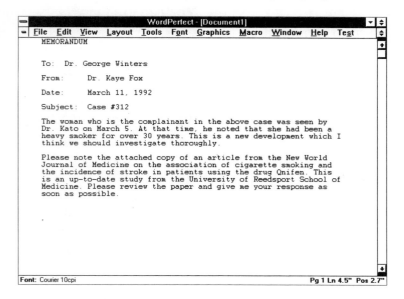

As each line of text reaches the right edge of the screen, the next word you type automatically moves to a new line. This process is called *word wrapping*, because the words "wrap" from one line to the next. Don't be concerned if the word wrapping on your screen doesn't exactly match ours. It simply means that you selected a different printer when you installed the program.

Word wrap

Moving Around the Document

In WordPerfect, you can move around a document in a variety of ways. The easiest way is to use the mouse to quickly move the insertion point anywhere in the document. Simply position the mouse pointer (which looks like an I-beam when it is in the Editing screen) at the desired location, and click the left mouse button to position the insertion point. To move to a location that is currently out of view, use the mouse and the scroll bar on the right side of the WordPerfect window to display the desired part of the document on the screen, and then click the mouse button to position the insertion point.

Clicking an insertion point

Moving with the keyboard →

You can also use the keyboard to move around a document. Try pressing the Up Arrow, Down Arrow, Left Arrow, and Right Arrow keys now. You can use these keys to move the insertion point up and down one line and left and right one character, respectively. Obviously, though, moving a line or character at a time is not the most efficient way to get around a document. Here are some faster ways:

To move the insertion point...	Press...
Left one word	Ctrl-Left Arrow
Right one word	Ctrl-Right Arrow
To end of a line	End
To beginning of line	Home
To beginning of line before codes	Home,Home
Up one paragraph	Ctrl-Up Arrow
Down one paragraph	Ctrl-Down Arrow
Up one screen	PgUp
Down one screen	PgDn
To top of previous page	Alt-PgUp
To top of next page	Alt-PgDn
To top of document	Ctrl-Home
To top of document before codes	Ctrl-Home,Ctrl-Home
To end of document after codes	Ctrl-End

Try using various keys and key combinations to move around the memo. When you're reasonably "mobile," rejoin us for a discussion of text selection techniques.

Key conventions

When two keys are separated by a hyphen (such as Ctrl-Left Arrow), press and hold down the first key, and then press the second key. When two or more keys are separated by commas (such as Home,Home), press and release each key in the order in which it appears in the instruction. ♦

CUA vs. 5.1 keyboards

When you installed Word-Perfect for Windows, the installation program asked whether you wanted to use the CUA (Common User Access) or the WordPerfect 5.1 keyboard layouts. In this book, we assume you are using the CUA keyboard layout. Here's how to switch from the CUA layout to 5.1: 1. From the File menu, choose Preferences and then Keyboard. 2. Click the Select button. 3. In the dialog box, select WPDOS51.WWK, and then click Select. 4. Click OK to return to the Editing screen. To switch from 5.1 to CUA, simply click the Default (CUA) button in the Keyboard dialog box, and then click OK.

Whichever keyboard layout you select, you can get information about keyboard shortcuts by choosing Keyboard from the Help menu. ♦

Selecting Text

Knowing how to select text efficiently saves you time, because you can then edit and apply formatting to blocks of text, instead of having to deal with individual characters. The simplest way to learn how to select text is to actually do it, so follow along as we demonstrate selecting text blocks of different shapes and sizes, first with the mouse:

1. Point to the first word of the first paragraph of the memo's message, and double-click the mouse button to select the word and the space after it. (You'll see the message *Select On* in the status bar.)

    Selecting words

2. Point to the word *development* in the last sentence of the same paragraph, and triple-click the mouse button to select the sentence containing that word.

    Selecting sentences

3. Point to a word in the second paragraph, and then quadruple-click (click four times) to select the entire paragraph.

    Selecting paragraphs

You don't have to select discreet units like words, sentences, or paragraphs. If you are skilled with your mouse, you can drag through the text itself to highlight exactly as much or as little as you need. You can also use your mouse in conjunction with the Shift key, like this:

Shift-clicking to select text

1. Click an insertion point just before the sentence that begins *This is an up-to-date.*

Clicking	**Double-clicking**	**Dragging**
You click the mouse button to position the insertion point, pull down menus, and select options. Clicking is simply a matter of quickly pressing and releasing the left mouse button once. ♦	You double-click to select options from menus and to select words in text. Double-clicking is similar to clicking, except that you quickly click the mouse button twice. Double-clicking is especially useful in lists, where the first click highlights the desired item on the list, and the second click initiates the command. ♦	Dragging across text highlights, or blocks, the text. Start by pointing to the character at one end of the text, and then hold down the left mouse button while moving the mouse. Release the button when all the desired text is highlighted. ♦

2. Point to the end of the second paragraph, hold down the Shift key, and click the mouse button. WordPerfect highlights the last two sentences of the memo.
3. Click anywhere in the memo to remove the highlight.

Now let's look at a couple of useful keyboard selection methods:

Select mode

1. Press the F8 function key to turn on Select mode. In the status bar, WordPerfect tells you that the mode is active.
2. Press the Right Arrow, Left Arrow, Up Arrow, and Down Arrow keys to select blocks of text of various shapes and sizes.
3. Try using several of the navigation key combinations listed in the table on page 6 in conjunction with Select mode to see their effects.
4. Press F8 again to turn off Select mode.

When Select mode is not turned on, you can use a variety of key combinations to highlight specific units of text. Here's a list of some of these units and the keys that select them:

To select...	Press...
A character	Shift-Left (or Right) Arrow
A word	Shift-Ctrl-Left (or Right) Arrow
Up one line	Shift-Up Arrow
Down one line	Shift-Down Arrow
To beginning of paragraph	Shift-Ctrl-Up Arrow
To end of paragraph	Shift-Ctrl-Down Arrow
To beginning of line	Shift-Home
To end of line	Shift-End
To beginning of document	Shift-Ctrl-Home
To end of document	Shift-Ctrl-End

Giving Instructions

Now that you can select text, you need to know how to tell WordPerfect what to do with the selection. You give Word-Perfect instructions in three ways: using menus, using keyboard shortcuts, and using the Button Bar and the Ruler.

Using the Menus

You can give WordPerfect instructions by means of commands that are arranged in menus on the menu bar at the top of the window. Because this procedure is the same for all Windows applications, we assume that you are familiar with it, and we provide only a quick review here. If you are a new Windows user, we suggest that you spend a little time becoming familiar with the mechanics of menus, commands, and dialog boxes before proceeding.

To choose a command from a menu, you first click the name of the menu in the menu bar. When the menu drops down, you simply click the name of the command you want. From the keyboard, you can press Alt to activate the menu bar and then press the underlined letter of the name of the menu you want. To move from one open menu to another, use the Left and Right Arrow keys. When you have located the command you want, press its underlined letter.

Choosing commands

Some command names are displayed in "gray" letters, indicating that you can't choose those commands. For example, the Paste command on the Edit menu appears in gray until you have used the Cut or Copy command, and the Cut and Copy commands appear in gray until you have selected some text.

Unavailable commands

Some command names are followed by an arrowhead (▶), indicating that choosing the command will display a submenu, called a *cascading menu*, from which you must choose a subcommand.

Cascading menus

Some command and subcommand names are followed by an ellipsis (...), indicating that you must supply more information before WordPerfect can carry out the command. When you choose one of these commands, WordPerfect displays a dialog box. You can then give the necessary information by typing in a text box or by selecting options from list boxes or groups of check boxes and option buttons. Clicking a command button closes the dialog box and carries out the command according to your specifications. Clicking Cancel closes the dialog box and also cancels the command. Some dialog boxes have command buttons that refine the original command or open other dialog boxes with more options.

Dialog boxes

Let's run through the steps for choosing a command and do some useful work at the same time:

1. Click View on the menu bar to display this menu:

The View menu provides commands for customizing the screen. We won't discuss these commands here. For now, let's focus on two of the commands that affect screen layout.

Displaying the Button Bar and Ruler

2. Choose the Button Bar command. WordPerfect displays the Button Bar across the top of the screen.

3. Next, choose the Ruler command from the View menu to turn on the Ruler. Your screen now looks like this:

Button Bar
Ruler

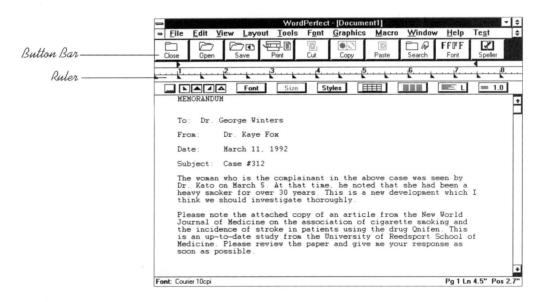

As we'll explain in a few minutes, the Button Bar and Ruler provide instant access to some of WordPerfect's most often used commands and options. When you are working with long documents, you might want to turn off these features so that you can display more of your text at one time. However, because choosing commands and options from the Button Bar and Ruler is often more efficient than going through the menus, we'll work with the Button Bar and Ruler turned on throughout the remainder of this book.

Many of WordPerfect's commands affect the appearance of your text. Let's try a few of these commands:

1. Point to the word *MEMORANDUM*, and double-click to highlight the entire word.

2. Choose the Bold command from the Font menu.

3. Drag across *To:* to select it, and again choose Bold from the Font menu.

4. Repeat step 3 with the From:, Date:, and Subject: headings. Here's the result:

Bold

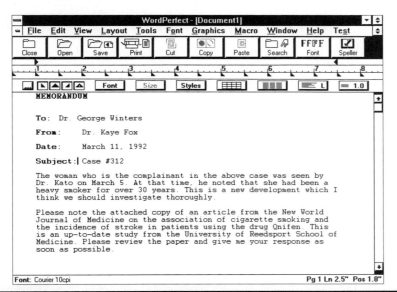

Keystroke shortcut

When you pull down a menu, notice that the keystrokes you press to carry out a particular command from the keyboard appear to the right of the command name. ♦

Quick cancel

You can press the Esc key to back out of commands or menus. For example, if you pull down the Font menu and then decide you don't want to choose one of its commands, simply press Esc to close the menu. You can also click anywhere outside the menu. ♦

Deleting attributes

The easiest way to delete an attribute is in the Reveal Codes screen, like this: **1.** Choose Reveal Codes from the View menu. **2.** Click the code for the attribute you want to delete (for example, [Bold On]). **3.** Press Del to delete the code. **4.** Choose Reveal Codes to return to the Editing screen. (See page 21 for more information.) ♦

The Bold command applies an *attribute*, also called a *format*, to the selected characters. Try applying a few more attributes:

Underline ———————→

1. Select *for over 30 years* in the first paragraph of the memo, and choose Underline from the Font menu.

Italic ———————→

2. Select *New World Journal of Medicine* in the second paragraph, and choose Italic from the Font menu.

Double Underline ———————→

3. Select *cigarette smoking*, and choose Double Underline from the Font menu.

Strikeout ———————→

4. Select *as soon as possible*, and choose Strikeout from the Font menu. Here are the results:

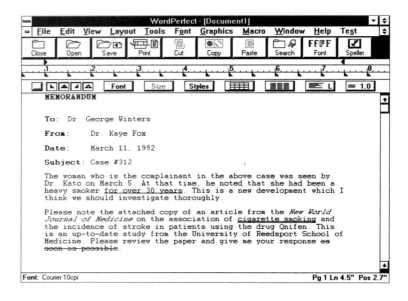

Striking out deletions

The Strikeout command can be useful when you're drafting contracts or legal reports for review by a second party and you want to show any deletions you have made. ♦

Redlining

You can use the Redline command on the Font menu to denote any additions you make to a document. Redlined text usually appears on a shaded background when it is printed. Used in conjunction with Strikeout, the Redline attribute is useful for printed documents, such as contracts, when you want changes to be visible. ♦

One-stop formatting

You can simultaneously apply several attributes to a text selection by choosing the Font command from the Font menu and making your selections in the Font dialog box (shown on page 17). For example, you can make text both bold and italic and increase its size by clicking the appropriate check boxes and then clicking OK. ♦

As you can see, choosing WordPerfect commands is not difficult. As you work your way through the examples in this book, you'll also become familiar with techniques for selecting options and specifying settings in dialog boxes.

Using Keyboard Shortcuts

If you prefer to use the keyboard, you can access many commands by means of keyboard shortcuts. WordPerfect's list of shortcuts is extensive, and it would take a lot of space to reproduce it here. You can display the list at any time simply by choosing the Keyboard command from the Help menu. (We talk more about WordPerfect's Help feature on page 30.)

Shortcut list

Using the Button Bar and the Ruler

The Button Bar and the Ruler both provide point-and-click ways of carrying out common word-processing tasks with the mouse. As you have seen, neither of them is displayed by default; you turn them on and off by choosing the Button Bar and Ruler commands from the View menu. Assuming that you turned them on in the previous section, let's look at each of them in turn.

The Button Bar   WordPerfect comes with a default Button Bar on which you'll find buttons that provide quick access to the commands WordPerfect Corporation thinks you'll use most frequently. The following table shows how you can access these commands through the menus:

Button/Command	Menu	Button/Command	Menu
Close	File	Copy	Edit
Open	File	Paste	Edit
Save	File	Search	Edit
Print	File	Font	Font
Cut	Edit	Speller	Tools

Equivalent menu commands

You can create your own Button Bars by assigning commands to buttons, arranging the buttons on a bar to suit your fancy, and then saving the custom Button Bar for future use. You can display the Button Bar across the top of your screen—the default position—or you can specify that it appear elsewhere. And your buttons can sport pictures, names, or both. Let's experiment:

Customizing the Button Bar

1. From the View menu, choose Button Bar Setup, and then choose Options. WordPerfect displays the dialog box shown here:

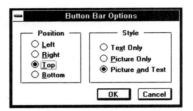

2. Select the Left and Text Only options, and click OK. The Button Bar, which no longer displays icons, moves to the left side of the screen:

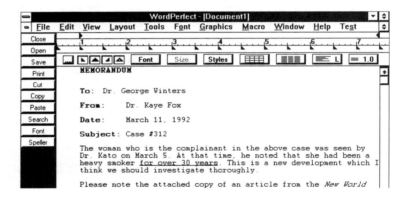

3. Choose Button Bar Setup and Options again, restore the original settings, and click OK.

You can also use the Button Bar Setup command to add new buttons to the menu bar. Follow these steps:

Adding buttons

1. From the View menu, choose Button Bar Setup and then Edit. WordPerfect displays this dialog box:

2. Move the pointer, which looks like a hand holding a card, to the File menu, and choose New. WordPerfect adds a New button at the right end of the Button Bar, scrolling the bar to the left so that the Close button is now out of sight.

3. Move the pointer over the New button, hold down the mouse button, drag the New button to the left end of the Button Bar, and release the mouse button. WordPerfect scrolls the bar to the right, and the Speller button is now out of sight, as you can see here:

You can scroll the Button Bar from left to right by clicking the arrows at the left end of the bar.

Scrolling the Button Bar

4. Click OK to close the dialog box.

To give an instruction using the Button Bar, you simply click the appropiate button. If WordPerfect needs more information before it can carry out the instruction, it displays a dialog box, just as if you had chosen the corresponding command from a menu. Let's test the New button:

Using the buttons

1. Click the New button on the Button Bar. WordPerfect opens a new document window.

2. Click the Close button. The document disappears without a trace.

Preserving old and new

To preserve the default Button Bar while at the same time saving your customized version, choose Button Bar Setup from the View menu, and then choose Save As from the cascading menu. Type a name for your Button Bar, and click Save. ◆

Displaying a different Button Bar

When you start a new WordPerfect session, the program loads the Button Bar that was active at the end of the previous session. To load a different Button Bar, choose Button Bar Setup from the View menu, then choose Select from the cascading menu, highlight the name of the Button Bar you want, and click Select. ◆

Predefined Button Bars

WordPerfect ships with several predefined Button Bars in addition to the default one (WP{WP}.WWB), including the Print Preview Button Bar (WP{WP}.PPB), the Table Button Bar (TABLES.WWB), the Figure Editor Button Bar (WP{WP}.FEB), the Equation Editor Button Bar (WP{WP}. EEB), and the Secondary Button Bar (SECOND.WWB). ◆

We won't take the time now to examine all the other buttons on the Button Bar. You'll have plenty of opportunities to use them throughout the book.

The Ruler   You use the Ruler as a quick way to set tabs; change the font and size of a text selection; apply a style; set up columns and tables; and change the margins, justification, and line spacing of a paragraph. You can perform all these tasks by choosing commands from menus, as shown in the following table, but clicking buttons and selecting options from the list boxes on the Ruler is usually more efficient.

Option	Menu	Command
Tabs	Layout	Line, Tab Set
Font	Font	Font
Size	Font	Font
Styles	Layout	Styles
Tables	Layout	Tables, Create
Columns	Layout	Columns, Define
Justification	Layout	Justification
Spacing	Layout	Line, Spacing

Equivalent menu commands

Let's see the effects produced by some of the options on the Ruler. First we'll adjust the tabs to control the alignment of the text in the memo's headings:

Setting tabs

1. We want the new tab settings to take effect from the first heading line, so click an insertion point in front of the *To:* heading.
2. Point to the tab marker (◣) at the 1.5-inch mark on the Ruler, hold down the mouse button, and then drag that marker to the left and out of sight. Do the same thing with the marker at the 2-inch mark.
3. Point to the Left Tab icon (the ◣ in the box), hold down the mouse button, and drag a tab marker to the 2.25-inch mark on the Ruler. As you can see, the text of the memo's headings is neatly aligned.

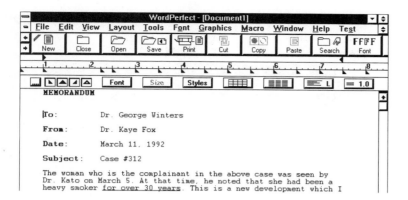

Now suppose we want to change the font of the memo. Changing the font of a document from the Ruler is simple once you have done some preliminary setup work. If you point to the Font button on the Ruler and hold down the mouse button now, you'll see only the Courier font listed. To make other fonts available from the Ruler, you have to add them to the Font list, like this:

1. Click the Font button on the Button Bar. WordPerfect displays a dialog box like this one:

Adding fonts to the Ruler

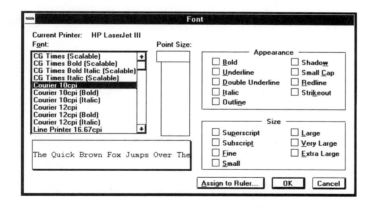

The fonts listed in the Font list box are those that are available for the printer you specified when you installed WordPerfect. We selected the Hewlett-Packard LaserJet III, which comes with the Times, Courier, Line Printer, and Univers fonts. (You have to scroll the list box to see the latter two fonts.)

2. Click the Assign To Ruler command button to display this Ruler Fonts Menu dialog box:

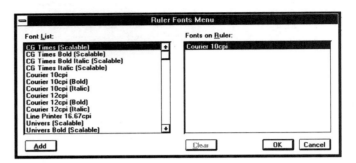

3. Select a font from the Font List box (we selected Times), and then click the Add button.
4. Select another font (Univers is a good choice if you have it), and then click Add again.
5. Click OK twice to return to the Editing screen.

Now let's see the effects of changing the font of the memo:

Changing fonts →

1. Move the insertion point to the top of the document, point to the Font button on the Ruler, and hold down the mouse button to display this list:

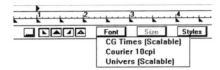

Formatting

We use the word *formatting* to refer to the shape, size, and general appearance of documents. Formatting can be applied to individual characters or words, as when you make them bold or underlined; individual paragraphs, as when you center a heading or change the line spacing; or the entire document, as when you change the margins. ♦

Formatting capabilities

You can add formatting to a document, but whether the formatting will print is a function of the capabilities of your printer and of the available fonts. For example, if the font you are using does not include italic, any italic formatting you specify will not print. The same is true if you change font sizes when the font you are using is available in only one size. ♦

Selecting a printer

If your printer's fonts don't appear in the list box in the Font or Ruler Fonts Menu dialog box, choose Select Printer from the File menu, and check that the correct printer is currently selected. If it isn't, select the correct one, and then click Select. The next time you choose Font, the Font list box should show the correct fonts. ♦

2. Drag to Univers, and release the mouse button. Word-
    Perfect reformats the entire document in that font.

3. Next, click an insertion point in front of the *To:* head-
    ing, and select Times from the Font list on the Ruler.
    WordPerfect formats the headings and text paragraphs
    of the memo in Times, leaving only the title in Univers.

Now suppose we want to make the title of the memo stand
out even more. Let's make it larger:

1. Point to the title, and double-click to select the word
    MEMORANDUM.

    Changing size

2. Point to the Size button on the Ruler, and hold down
    the mouse button to display this list of size options:

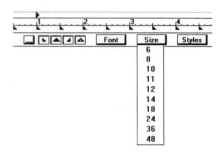

3. Drag to 18, and release the mouse button. WordPerfect
    instantly changes the size of the selected text.

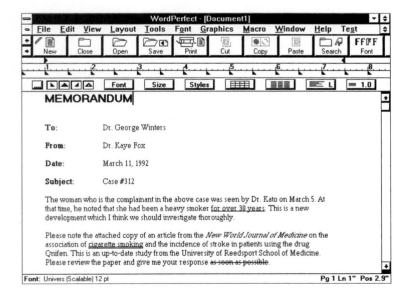

Now let's turn our attention to the other end of the Ruler and see what the memo looks like if we change the justification. The way you justify, or align, your text affects the way it looks and can determine its impact. The word *justification* means to arrange lines of text in such a way that all the lines come out even at one or both of the margins. WordPerfect offers four justification types: Left, Right, Center, and Full.

When you start WordPerfect, left justification is the default, meaning that the lines are even at the left margin but uneven at the right, as they are in the memo. With right justification, the lines are even at the right margin and uneven at the left margin. With centered justification, the lines are centered between the left and right margins. And with full justification, the lines are even at both the left and right margins.

If you want to change the justification, you can make the change before or after you type the text. Follow these steps to apply full justification to the paragraphs of the memo:

Changing justification

1. Click an insertion point at the beginning of the memo's first text paragraph, in front of the word *The*.
2. Point to the Justification button, and hold down the mouse button to display these options:

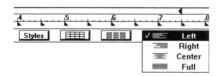

Justifying before typing

When you start a new document on a clean Editing screen, you can change the justification before you begin typing by following step 2 above and then selecting one of the options from the Justification list. ♦

Justification options

You center an entire document with the Center justification option, and you center a paragraph or a selected block of text with the Center feature (see page 69). However, as soon as you press Enter, the Center feature is turned off.

Similarly, you right-align an entire document with the Right justification option, and you right-align a single line of text with the Flush Right feature. If you want to right-align multiple lines with Flush Right, you must select the lines first.

When you have turned on right or center justification, you cannot use either the Center or the Flush Right feature. ♦

3. Drag to Full, and release the mouse button. Word-
    Perfect makes the lines of the two text paragraphs even
    at both margins.

4. Now suppose you want to center the memo title. Point
    to the word *MEMORANDUM*, and double-click to select
    the title. Then select Center from the Justification list.
    Here's the result:

Centering text

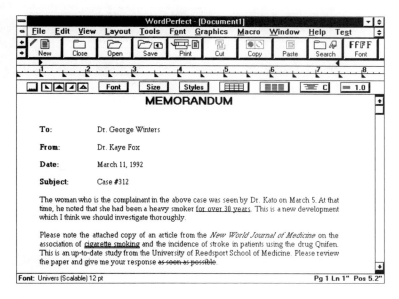

As you have seen, the Ruler provides some powerful
shortcuts for manipulating the appearance of your document.
Before we go any further, we need to talk a bit about the
codes WordPerfect uses to implement your selections.

Taking a Look at WordPerfect's Codes

If you're a veteran WordPerfect user, you'll be happy to
know that you can still access the Reveal Codes screen in
WordPerfect for Windows. Here, we'll explain the concept
for new WordPerfect users. Whenever you apply a format,
such as center justification or the Bold attribute, WordPerfect
inserts a code in your document. These codes determine the
way your document looks both on the screen and when
printed. You cannot see the codes in the normal Editing
screen, but you can see them in the Reveal Codes screen. If
applying a format doesn't produce quite the result you were

expecting, you can check the position of your formatting codes by activating this screen. Here's how to display the Reveal Codes screen.

Displaying the Reveal Codes screen

1. Choose Reveal Codes from the View menu. The screen splits in two, with the memo displayed in both halves, as shown here:

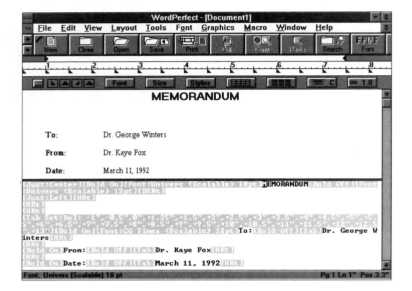

The normal Editing screen occupies the top half of the screen, and the Reveal Codes screen occupies the bottom half. You can move the cursor, which is a solid block, around the Reveal Codes screen just as you would move the insertion point around the Editing screen.

Notice the codes such as [Just:Center], [Bold On], and [Bold Off], which WordPerfect inserted when you formatted the memo. Paired codes, such as those for bold, have on and off components. Other formats, such as those for justification, are turned on by one code and remain in effect until a different code changes the format. You'll also notice Hard Return codes ([HRt]), which WordPerfect inserts when you press Enter, and Soft Return codes ([SRt]), which indicate line breaks caused by word wrapping. (They are called soft returns because your editing changes their positions.)

Don't be intimidated by all the coding. If you are like most people, when you get used to the codes, you'll think nothing of flipping between the Editing screen and the Reveal Codes screen. We'll return to the Reveal Codes screen periodically throughout the book to help you become more familiar with WordPerfect's formatting codes. For now, let's return to the normal Editing screen:

1.   From the View menu, choose Reveal Codes again.

Saving Documents

You probably know that the memo you have typed currently exists in your computer's memory and that this memory (called RAM for *random access memory*) is temporary. All information in RAM is wiped out when you turn off the computer. To move the memo to a more permanent storage place, you have to save it.

When you tell WordPerfect to save a document, the pro-   *Naming files*
gram asks you to supply a filename. Using up to eight characters, you should try to come up with a name that bears some relationship to the document you're saving. And you should be consistent. For example, you might want to assign similar names to documents connected with the same project so that they are readily identifiable as part of that project.

Enough lecturing. Let's save the memo:

1.   With the memo displayed on your screen, click the Save button. WordPerfect then displays the Save As dialog box, shown on the next page.

Filename characters

Here's a list of the characters you can use in filenames:

    A-Z
    0-9
    ! @ # $ % & ( ) - ' ' { }^

WordPerfect does not accept these characters in filenames:

    * + = [ ] : ; " ~ < > ? \ ,

and you cannot use the space character. You can use periods only in conjunction with a filename extension. ♦

Filename extensions

To further identify the contents of a file, you can add a filename extension of up to three characters. For example, you might use the extensions LET (for letters) and MEM (for memos). Do not use BAT, COM, or EXE; these extensions are reserved for files that contain programs. WordPerfect reserves the extensions WCM and WWK for special files. ♦

Saving with a new name

After you've given a document a name, WordPerfect saves the document with that name unless you tell it otherwise. To change the name, choose Save As from the File menu, and specify a new name. WordPerfect then saves the current version of the document under the new name while preserving the previous version under the old name. ♦

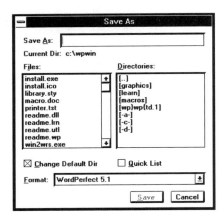

2. In the Save As text box, type a filename and an extension (use *qnifen.mem* for this example), and then click Save. WordPerfect saves the file in the C:\WPWIN directory.

The memo remains on your screen so that you can continue working on it. The next time you click the Save button to save your changes, WordPerfect saves the file without displaying the Save As dialog box, because you've already given the memo a name.

Backing Up Files

To spare you the trauma of losing work because of machine failures or power outages, or because you unintentionally delete a file, you should regularly *back up*, or make copies of, your files. While you are creating a document, you can back it up by selecting the Original Document Backup option and then saving the file regularly. Or you can have WordPerfect automatically back up your files by using the Timed Document Backup option. We discuss both methods in this section.

Retaining the Previous Version of a Document

By using the Original Document Backup option to change the extension of the previous version of a document to BK!, you can save both the current and previous versions. WordPerfect stores the backup file in the same directory as the current version.

Let's use the QNIFEN.MEM file as an example. To use the Original Document Backup option:

1. From the File menu, choose Preferences, and then
    choose Backup. WordPerfect displays this dialog box:

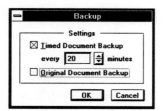

2. Select Original Document Backup, and click OK.
3. Now save QNIFEN.MEM by clicking the Save button.
    WordPerfect renames the version of the memo that is
    stored on disk QNIFEN.BK!, and the current version
    becomes QNIFEN.MEM.

The next time you save QNIFEN.MEM, WordPerfect will
delete QNIFEN.BK!, save QNIFEN.MEM as QNIFEN.BK!, and
then save the new version of the memo as QNIFEN.MEM.
Then if QNIFEN.MEM is damaged or deleted, you can re-   *Recovering a file*
trieve QNIFEN.BK!, rename it QNIFEN.MEM, and recon-
struct any changes you have made since the last time you
saved the document.

Making Timed Backups

By default, WordPerfect's Timed Document Backup option
is turned on and is set to save your work every 20 minutes.
If you are working with more than one document, Word-
Perfect creates a backup file for each one (WP{WP}.BK1
for document 1, WP{WP}.BK2 for document 2, and so on up
to WP{WP}.BK9). Backup files are stored in the main Word-
Perfect for Windows directory (WPWIN) unless you specify
another directory. If you lose the current version of your
work because of a power or system failure, you can retrieve
the backup file and pick up where you left off. However, if
you end your current work session normally, WordPerfect
deletes the backup files.

If you decide that 20 minutes is too long an interval   *Changing the*
between backups, you can change the interval as follows: *timed backup*
                                                                    interval

1. From the File menu, choose Preferences, and then
    choose Backup to display the Backup dialog box.

2. Check that the Timed Document Backup option is selected (that its check box contains an X).

3. Change the setting in the Every edit box to the desired time, and click OK.

Retrieving Existing Documents

To give you some practice in retrieving documents, let's open the QNIFEN.BK! file that WordPerfect created when you last saved the memo. Follow these steps:

Opening documents

1. Click the Open button on the Button Bar. WordPerfect displays a dialog box like this one:

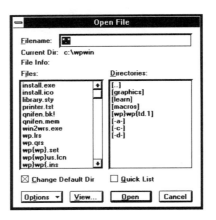

The filenames in the Files list box are those that are stored in the directory specified next to Current Dir.

Using the Quick List

WordPerfect's Quick List is a list of the directories you use most often. You can display the Quick List from any dialog box that requires you to enter a filename, such as the Open File and Save As dialog boxes. You can then access files in those directories without having to click your way through long lists or type cumbersome pathnames. To use the Quick List:

1. Open a dialog box that has the Quick List option (known as directory dialog boxes). **2.** With the Quick List option selected, click the Edit Quick List button, and then click Add. **3.** In the Add Quick List Item dialog box, enter the directory name (for example, *c:\wpwin\files*). You can also click the List button (the button with the file-folder icon) to display a list of your directories and then select from the list. **4.** Enter a name for the directory in the Descriptive Name text box. This name will appear in the Quick List box, so make it as descriptive as you can. **5.** Click OK to close the Add Quick List Item dialog box, and then click OK in the Edit Quick List dialog box to save the Quick List. **6.** Now all you have to do to access files in the C:\WPWIN\FILES directory is click the descriptive name in the Quick List list box. ♦

2. If the file you want is not stored in the current directory, you need to switch to the correct directory in order to select the file. Double-click a directory name in the Directories list box to display its files in the Files list box and its subdirectories in the Directories list box. Double-click a subdirectory to display its files and sub-directories, and so on.

Switching directories

3. When you have located QNIFEN.BK!, select it, and click Open. WordPerfect loads the previous version of the memo in its own document window.

Notice that the Ruler does not appear in the QNIFEN.BK! document window. To display the Ruler, simply choose Ruler from the View menu. If you want the Ruler to appear automatically in all future windows, follow these steps:

1. Choose Preferences from the File menu, and then choose Environment.

Displaying the Ruler in all windows

2. In the Ruler Section of the Environment Settings dialog box, select the Automatic Ruler Display option, and then click OK to close the dialog box and return to the Editing screen.

You can, of course, turn off the Ruler at any time by choosing Ruler from the View menu.

Creating New Documents

You now have two documents open on your screen, though QNIFEN.MEM is totally obscured by QNIFEN.BK!. For good measure, let's open a third document, this time a brand new one. Follow these steps:

1. Choose New from the File menu (or click the New button you added earlier to the Button Bar).

That's all there is to it. A new blank document is displayed in a window, on top of QNIFEN.MEM and QNIFEN.BK!.

Manipulating Windows

Now that we have a few windows to play with, we'll pause here to review some window basics. Being able to work with more than one document open at a time is useful, especially if you need to use the same information in different documents. For example, you might use the same text in a memo, in a letter, and in a legal brief. Follow these steps to see how easy it is to move from one document to another.

1. Click Window on the menu bar to display this menu:

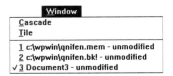

   As you can see, the three open documents are listed at the bottom of the menu, with a check mark beside the active document.

2. Choose QNIFEN.MEM from the list of open documents. WordPerfect brings the current version of the memo to the top of the stack of windows.

*Arranging
windows*

3. Choose Tile from the Window menu. WordPerfect arranges the three open documents so that they each occupy about a third of the screen, like this:

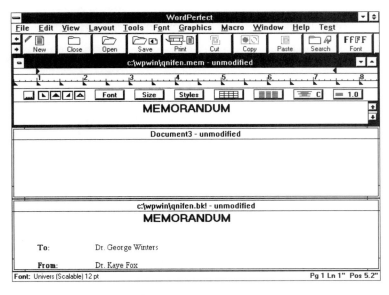

*Activating a
window*

4. Click anywhere in QNIFEN.BK! to activate it. Notice that the title bar of the active document is a different color from the other two title bars and that scroll bars

appear only in the active window. Any entries you make and any commands you choose will affect only the active document.

5. Click the Maximize button (the upward-pointing arrowhead in the top-right corner of the QNIFEN.BK! window). QNIFEN.BK! expands to fill the screen, completely obscuring the other two documents.

Expanding a window

6. Choose Open from the File menu, and again select QNIFEN.BK! and click Open. WordPerfect opens a window that displays a second copy of QNIFEN.BK!. (Opening two copies of the same document lets you view different parts at the same time.)

Viewing one file in two windows

7. Verify that you have two copies of the same document open by clicking Window on the menu bar. At the bottom of the menu, a second version of QNIFEN.BK! is listed. Close the menu by clicking outside it.

These simple techniques work equally well no matter how many documents you have open. (You can have nine documents open at one time, but we've found that three is the practical limit if you want to be able to see them all at the same time and do useful work.)

Closing Documents

When you've finished working with a document, it's wise to close it to conserve your computer's memory for the work at hand. In this section, we'll show you one way to close one copy of QNIFEN.BK!, another to close the other copy of QNIFEN.BK!, and yet another to close the blank document.

1. With QNIFEN.BK! still active, choose Close from the Document Control menu at the left end of the window's menu bar (*not* its title bar). WordPerfect closes the document.

2. With QNIFEN.BK! active, click the Close button on the Button Bar. (If you have made changes, WordPerfect asks whether to save the document. Click No.)

3. Activate the blank document, and choose Close from the File menu. (Again, click No if you're asked about saving changes.)

The current version of the memo is now the only document open on your screen.

Getting Help

With WordPerfect for Windows, help is never far away. If you get stuck, you have several options, depending on what level of information you need. At the "memory jogger" end of the spectrum is the document window's status bar, which gives a brief explanation of the highlighted command, and at the other end is the comprehensive reference manual. In between is WordPerfect's Help feature, which we'll briefly look at here.

The Help Feature

WordPerfect for Windows' Help feature gives you on-the-spot information about the program's features and options and how to use them. You access the information by choosing commands from the Help menu at the right end of the menu bar. The type of information displayed depends on which command you choose and what you are doing in WordPerfect at the time.

The best way to explore the Help feature is to have WordPerfect itself show you around. Here's how to ask for a guided tour:

1. Click Help on the menu bar to display this menu:

2. Choose Using Help to display this Help window:

3. Read the information in the window, and then click the Using Help button on the left. WordPerfect takes you to the Help window that explains how to use the Index, Back, Backward Browse, Forward Browse, and Search buttons at the top of the window.

4. Point to the Index button in the Help window, and hold down the mouse button to display a pop-up window with information about the Index button. (Clicking the button flashes a white box on the screen; the information is only visible while the mouse button is down.)

5. Point to each button in turn, and hold down the mouse button to give yourself an idea of how Help works.

6. Now click the Back button on the Help window Button Bar to return to the first Help window. Then click the Help Menu button, and browse through the information in the Help Menu window.

7. When you are ready, choose Exit from the window's File menu to close the Help window.

Until you become familiar with WordPerfect for Windows, you'll probably find yourself calling on the Help feature frequently. It's concise explanations will usually be all you need to get you over any stumbling blocks.

Customer Support

If WordPerfect's Help feature can't answer your question, you can call WordPerfect's Customer Support. If you are a WordPerfect for Windows user within the United States or Canada, you can call Monday through Friday from 7 AM to 6 PM Mountain time. When you call Customer Support, you should be within reach of your computer, and you should have your registration number in hand.

The following is a list of Customer Support departments and their corresponding toll-free numbers:

Installation	(800) 228-6076
Features	(800) 228-1029
Graphics/Table/Equations	(800) 228-6013
Macros/Merge/Labels	(800) 228-1032
Laser/PostScript Printers	(800) 228-1023
Dot-Matrix/All Other Printers	(800) 228-1017
Networks	(800) 228-6066
After Regular Hours	(801) 228-9908

2

Business Letters

Adding a Date code
Page 62

Replacing text
Page 42

Print Preview
Page 53

Fox & Associates
Medical Malpractice Consultants
1224 Evergreen Road
Lake Oswego, OR 97035

March 25, 1992

Mr. David Robertson
Sullivan, Duffy and Bridge, Attorneys at
145 Salmon St.
Portland, OR 97201

RE: Case #312, Rebecca Brand v. Midvalle

Dear Mr. Robertson:

Dr. George Winters and I have reviewe t
above case thoroughly and have come to
that Rebecca Brand's stroke may have bee
of the drug Qnifan. However, in her case
have been equally or more important.

Recent case reports have associated str
administration over several years. Pati
frequently also taking many other drugs
association of stroke with these drugs
has not been documented.

The other risk factors tha
Rebecca Brand's stroke are

1. She is more than 59 yea
2. She has smoked cigarett
3. She has mald hypertensi
Age, smoking, and hyperten
stroke.

I hope this summary of our
call upon me for further i

Sincerely,

Kaye E. Fox, Ph.D.

WordPerfect - [case312.let - Print Preview]

File   View   Pages   Window   Help

Close
Print
Full Page
FacingPg
Prev Page
Next Page

8.5" x 11"

Fox & Associates
Medical Malpractice Consultants
1224 Evergreen Road
Lake Oswego, OR 97035

March 25, 1992

Mr. David Robertson
Sullivan, Duffy and Bridge, Attorneys at Law
145 Salmon St.
Portland, OR 97201

RE: Case #312, Rebecca Brand vs. Midvalley Clinic

Dear Mr. Robertson:

Dr. George Winters and I have thoroughly reviewed the medical files in the
above case and have come to an opinion. We conclude that Rebecca Brand's
stroke may have been exacerbated by her use of the drug Qnifen. However, in
her case other risk factors may have been equally or more important.

The other risk factors that may have also played a role in Rebecca Brand's
stroke are the following:

    1. She is more than 59 years old.

    2. She has smoked cigarettes for over 25 years.

    3. She has mild hypertension.

Age, smoking, and hypertension are well-known risk factors for stroke.

Recent case reports have associated stroke with Qnifen administration over a
number of years. Patients taking Qnifen are frequently also taking many other
drugs. However, the association of stroke with these drugs in the absence of
Qnifen has not been documented.

I hope this summary of our opinion will be of help to you. Please call upon me
for further information should you require it.

Sincerely,

Kaye E. Fox, Ph.D.

Increasing margins
Page 49

Starting a spell-check
Page 44

Double-spacing
Page 51

Changing fonts
Page 46

Whether you're writing letters for business or personal use, WordPerfect can simplify the entire process by making light work of tasks such as editing, detecting and correcting spelling errors, and adjusting margins and line spacing. In this chapter, we build on what you learned in Chapter 1 and show you how to prepare and print a professional-looking letter using some familiar features and some new ones.

The letter we use for the examples in this chapter is shown on the facing page. Start by typing the letter or one of your own. To follow along, you must include misspellings, double words (such as *the the*), and mixed-up cases (such as *PLease*), and you should include a numbered list. Be sure to press the Enter key to add any necessary blank lines. If at any time you want to start over, simply click the Close button on the Button Bar, and click No when WordPerfect asks whether to save your changes. When you have finished typing the letter, save it with the name CASE312.LET by clicking Save on the Button Bar, typing *case312.let* in the Save As dialog box, and then pressing Enter.

Fine-Tuning the Letter's Contents

Ensuring accuracy

Before you modify the way any document looks, you should be sure it accurately says what you want it to say. If you spend time formatting a letter so that it fits on one page and then make major content changes, such as adding a paragraph, your formatting efforts might be wasted. In this section, the changes you'll make are small, but they are significant in terms of the impression your letter will make on its readers. First we discuss some simple editing techniques, and then we show you how to use the powerful Search and Replace features. We finish off the section by putting the Speller program through its paces. With these skills, you'll be able to mop up errors and fix inconsistencies in no time, and you can then turn your attention to formatting.

Editing Basics

Correcting mistakes without creating a mess is one of the big advantages that word processors have over typewriters. With WordPerfect, you have several ways to make corrections,

```
Fox & Associates
Medical Malpractice Consultants
1224 Evergreen Road
Lake Oswego, OR 97035

March 25, 1992

Mr. David Robertson
Sullivan, Duffy and Bridge, Attorneys at Law
145 Salmon St.
Portland, OR 97201

RE: Case #312, Rebecca Brand v. Midvalley Clinic

Dear Mr. Robertson:

Dr. George Winters and I have reviewe the medical files in the
above case thoroughly and have come to an opinion. We conclude
that Rebecca Brand's stroke may have been exacerbated by her use
of the drug Qnifan. However, in her case other risk factors may
have been equally or more important.

Recent case repurts have associated stroke with Qnifan
administration over several years. Patient's taking Qnifan are
frequently also taking many other drugs; however, the the
association of stroke with these drugs in the absence of Qnifan
has not been documented.

The other risk factors that may have also played a role in
Rebecca Brand's stroke are the following:

1. She is more than 59 years old.
2. She has smoked cigarettes for over 30 years.
3. She has mald hypertension.
Age, smoking, and hypertension are well-known risk factors for
stroke.

I hope this summary of our opinion will be of help to you. PLease
call upon me for further information should you require it.

Sincerely,


Kaye E. Fox, Ph.D.
```

which we'll cover here. But before we get going, we need to be sure we are all using the same terminology. In this book, we use the word *delete* to mean *erase completely*—for example, you delete a word you no longer want in your text. We use the word *cut* to mean *erase* with the intention of inserting the text somewhere else. Deleting text is a one-step process; cutting text is the first step in a process that actually moves the text rather than erasing it completely.

Deleting Text   You are probably already familiar with the Backspace key (←), which deletes the character to the left of the insertion point. To delete the character to the right of the insertion point, you use the Del (Delete) key. Try using Del to correct a small error in the letter:

1. Click an insertion point in front of the apostrophe in *Patient's* in the second paragraph.
2. Press the Del key to delete the apostrophe.

That's all there is to it. You can delete more than one character at a time by selecting the text you want to delete—such as a word, line, or entire paragraph—and then pressing Backspace or Del. You can press Ctrl-Backspace to delete the word containing the insertion point and Ctrl-Del to delete the text from the insertion point to the end of the line.

If you select a block of text and begin typing, WordPerfect deletes the selection and replaces it with whatever you type. The selection and the replacement don't have to be the same size. Try this:

1. Point to the word *several* in the second paragraph, and double-click to select the word.
2. Type *a number of*. WordPerfect replaces the seven characters in *several* with the eleven characters in *a number of*, pushing the existing text to the right to make room.

Overtyping Errors　　Another way to correct minor errors is to overtype them. Follow these steps, noticing the difference between this example and the previous one:

1. Click an insertion point between the *v* and the period of the abbreviation for *versus* in the *RE:* heading.
2. Type an *s*. Predictably, WordPerfect inserts the character at the insertion point.
3. Now click an insertion point between the *s* and the semicolon (;) at the end of the word *drugs* in the second paragraph.
4. Press the Ins key to switch to Typeover mode, and type a period, a space, and a capital *H*. WordPerfect substitutes these three characters for the existing three characters.
5. Click an insertion point before *30* in the numbered list.
6. Type *25*. WordPerfect overtypes the existing number with the new number.
7. Press the Ins key again to stop overtyping.

The last step is very important if you don't want to overtype text inadvertently.

Deleting shortcuts

Typeover mode

Moving Text   When it comes to rearranging text, Word-Perfect's cut-and-paste technique couldn't be easier. It lets you move words, sentences, and paragraphs in just a few simple steps. Let's give it a try:

1. Point anywhere in the second paragraph of the letter, and quadruple-click the mouse button (click four times) to select the entire paragraph.

2. Click the Cut button on the Button Bar. (This button is dimmed and unavailable if no text is highlighted.) WordPerfect cuts the highlighted paragraph from the letter and moves it to a temporary storage place in your computer's memory called the Clipboard.

Cutting text

3. Click an insertion point just before the paragraph that begins *I hope this summary*.

4. Click the Paste button on the Button Bar. (This button is available only when something has been previously cut or copied.) Here's the paragraph in its new location:

Pasting text

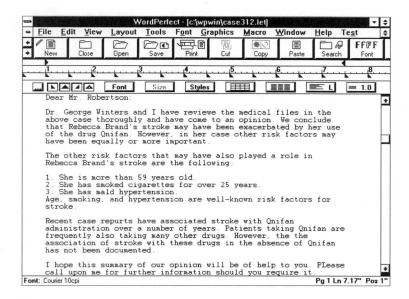

Copying Text   Copying text from one part of your document to another is as easy as moving it. Again, the process involves two buttons—this time Copy and Paste—and again Word-Perfect uses the Clipboard as an intermediary storage place. For practice, we'll copy one of the paragraphs in the letter, but instead of pasting the copy elsewhere in the same document, we'll copy it to a different document:

1. Click an insertion point just before the paragraph that begins *The other risk factors*, hold down the Shift key, and click after the paragraph that ends *factors for stroke*. WordPerfect highlights this block of text:

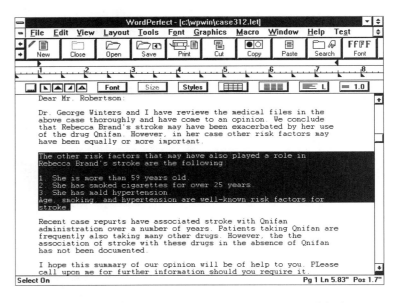

Copying text →

2. Click the Copy button on the Button Bar. (This button is available only when text is highlighted.) WordPerfect moves a copy of the text to the Clipboard.
3. Choose New from the File menu to open a new blank document.

The Clipboard

The Windows Clipboard is a temporary storage place used to hold cut or copied data from all Windows applications. It can also be used to transfer data from the documents of one application to those of another. ♦

Temporary storage

Because the Windows Clipboard is a temporary storage space, exiting Windows or turning off your computer erases any information that is stored there, unless you save the Clipboard file. See the Windows documentation for more information. ♦

Highlighting spaces

When you highlight and move or copy text, you need to pay attention to the spaces at the beginning and/or end of the highlighted selection. Otherwise, you may end up with too many spaces in some places and not enough in others. With practice, you'll soon be able to judge which spaces to include in the selection. ♦

4. Click the Paste button on the Button Bar. WordPerfect inserts the copy of the selection at the top of the new document.

5. Click the Close button on the Button Bar to close the new document, clicking No when WordPerfect asks whether to save your changes.

Pasting into a different document

You could now open another new document and paste another copy of the selection. As long as you do not cut or copy something else to the Clipboard, the selection remains there for use wherever you need it.

Undoing Editing Mistakes   If you make a mistake at any point in an editing procedure, you can correct the error by choosing Undo from the Edit menu. Choosing Undo reverses your previous action, restoring the text exactly as it was. For example, if you choose Undo after pasting the selection in the new document, WordPerfect erases the selection. (It is still stored on the Clipboard, however.)

WordPerfect also has a command that is specifically designed for restoring deleted text. If you accidentally delete the wrong thing, don't panic: The Undelete command is only a couple of mouse clicks away.

When it comes to reversing an accidental deletion, the difference between the Undo and the Undelete commands is that Undo restores the deletion to its original location, whereas Undelete restores it to the location of the insertion point. Try this:

1. Point to the word *thoroughly* in the first paragraph of the letter, and double-click to select it.

2. Press Del to delete the entire word.

3. Click an insertion point anywhere in the document, and then choose Undo from the Edit menu. WordPerfect restores the deleted word to its original location no matter where the insertion point is.

Reversing an editing command

4. Now select the word *thoroughly* again, and press Del.

Undeleting a deletion

5. Click an insertion point in front of the misspelled word *reviewe*, and choose Undelete from the Edit menu. WordPerfect inserts *thoroughly* in front of *reviewe*, highlights it, and displays this dialog box:

6. Click the Restore button to restore the deletion to its new location.

WordPerfect stores your last three deletions. If the highlighted deletion is not the one you want, you can click the Previous and Next buttons in the Undelete dialog box to display the other stored deletions. Click Restore when the one you want is highlighted in your document.

Searching for and Replacing Text

With the Search feature, you can move quickly to any location in a document by giving WordPerfect a word, phrase, or code (called the search string) that you want to find. You use the Replace feature in conjunction with the Search feature to replace a specific word, phrase, or code with a new word, phrase, or code.

Let's use the Search feature in the CASE312.LET document to locate the word *Qnifan*:

Case counts	Directing your search	Selecting text with search
When you use the Search or Replace commands, keep in mind that using lowercase letters in your search string matches both lowercase and uppercase letters, whereas using uppercase letters matches only uppercase letters. For example, the search string *cat* finds *cat* and *Cat*, but the search string *Cat* finds only *Cat*. ♦	You can change the direction of your search while the Search dialog box is displayed on your screen by changing the Direction option from Forward to Backward and vice versa. ♦	You can use Search to select a block of text. Here's how: **1.** With the insertion point at the beginning of the text block, press F8 to turn on Select mode, and then press F2 (the Search keyboard shortcut). **2.** In the Search dialog box, enter a search string in the Search For text box, and click Search. The text is highlighted to the first occurrence of the string. ♦

1. Move the insertion point to the beginning of the letter.
2. Click the Search button on the Button Bar to display this dialog box:

Searching for text

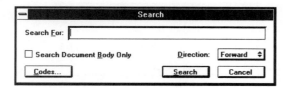

3. Type *Qnifan* in the Search For text box, and click the Search button. WordPerfect instantly moves the insertion point to just after the first occurrence of *Qnifan*, as shown here:

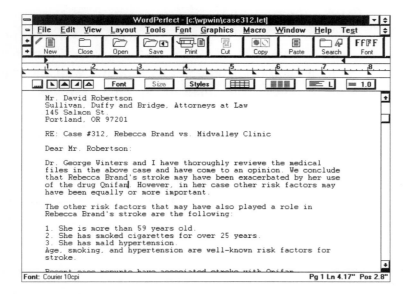

4. Choose Search Next from the Edit menu to find the second occurrence of *Qnifan*.
5. Now choose Search Previous from the Edit menu to move back to the first occurrence.

If you followed along with the memo example in Chapter 1, you know that the word *Qnifan* should actually be *Qnifen*. You can quickly correct this error by using the Replace feature.

1. Move the insertion point to the beginning of the document by pressing Ctrl-Home.

Replacing text

2. Choose Replace from the Edit menu. WordPerfect displays this dialog box:

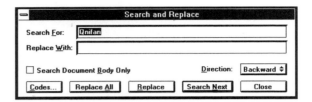

3. The word *Qnifan* is still in the Search For text box, so click the Replace With text box, and type *Qnifen*.
4. Choosing Search Previous earlier changed the Direction setting to Backward, so select Forward from the Direction drop-down list box.
5. We want WordPerfect to replace all instances of the search string with the replace string, so click Replace All. If you click Replace instead, WordPerfect will stop at each occurrence of *Qnifan* and wait for you to confirm the replacement by clicking Replace.
6. Click Close to close the dialog box.

Let's check that all the *Qnifans* have changed to *Qnifens*:

1. Move the insertion point back to the beginning of the letter.
2. Click the Search button on the Button Bar. The word *Qnifan* should still appear in the Search For text box.

No-confirmation caution

Be careful when using Replace All to replace text. If you accidentally misspell the replacement text, the results could be disastrous. If you catch the error prior to performing any other editing action, you can use the Undo command to reverse the effects of the Replace command. ♦

Code searching and replacing

To search for and replace codes, such as [Bold On], follow these steps: **1.** Choose Replace from the Edit menu. **2.** Click the Codes button to display the Codes dialog box. **3.** In the Search Codes list box, press the Down Arrow key until the code you want to search for is highlighted. **4.** Press Enter to insert the code in the Search For text box. **5.** Click the Replace With text box, and then repeat steps 2, 3, and 4 to insert the replacement code. **6.** Click the Replace or Replace All button. For more information see page 84. ♦

3. Click Search in the dialog box. If all instances of *Qnifan* are now *Qnifen*, WordPerfect briefly displays a *String not found* message in the bottom-left corner of the screen, and the dialog box closes.
4. Save the letter by clicking Save on the Button Bar.

With all four *Qnifens* in place, the letter looks like this:

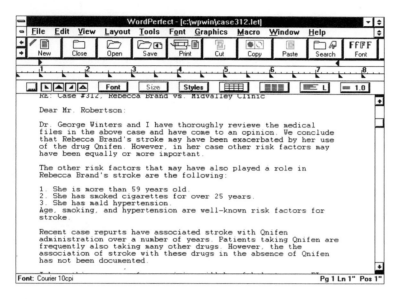

Checking Spelling

Nobody spells or types perfectly all the time. Fortunately, WordPerfect's Speller program not only detects spelling errors, but also catches double words and inappropriate capitalization. What's more, the Speller is so easy to use that you'll have no excuse for not using it on every document you create in WordPerfect.

The Speller works by comparing the words in your document with the words in its dictionary. If it can't find a matching word in its dictionary, it displays a list of alternative spellings. (If the Speller has no alternative spellings for a word, a *Not Found* message appears in the bottom-left corner of the dialog box.) You can select a replacement word from the list or edit the word yourself. You can also tell WordPerfect to skip over any other occurrences of that word in your document, or you can type the word in the text box as you would like it to appear in your document.

The Speller doesn't stop for many common names, but it will pause for unusual names, such as *Sullivan* and *Rebecca.* If the name is spelled correctly, you can tell the Speller not to stop for that name again, or you can add the name to a supplementary dictionary that WordPerfect will then use in addition to its main dictionary (see tip below).

If you did not install the Speller files when you installed WordPerfect, you must do so before continuing with the examples in this chapter. Then, with the letter displayed on your screen, follow these steps to check your spelling:

1. Move the insertion point to the beginning of the letter by pressing Ctrl-Home.

Starting a spell-check

2. Click the Speller button on the Button Bar. (If you created the New button in Chapter 1, you'll have to scroll the Button Bar to the left to see the Speller button.) WordPerfect displays the Speller dialog box, as shown here:

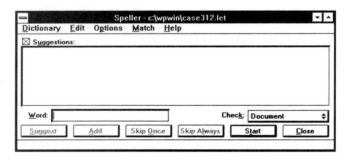

Adding words to a supplementary dictionary

If you frequently use jargon that is common in your business, or if you regularly communicate with the same people, you can add the jargon words or proper names to a supplementary dictionary that Word will check in addition to its main dictionary when spell-checking a document. All you have to do is click the Add button at the bottom of the Speller dialog box when WordPerfect displays the word or name in the Word text box. ♦

Spell-checking a selection or word

If you select a block of text before choosing Speller from the Tools menu, by default WordPerfect checks only the selection. You can also select Word from the Check drop-down list box on the right side of the Speller dialog box to check the spelling of the word containing the insertion point. ♦

Notice that, by default, WordPerfect will check the spelling of the entire document. You can change this selection, but for now leave it as it is.

3. Click the Start button.

4. When the Speller stops on *Sullivan*, *Rebecca*, *vs.*, and *Midvalley*, click the Skip Always button to tell Word-Perfect to ignore these words even though they are not in its dictionary.

   Proper names

5. When the Speller stops on the word *reviewe*, double-click *reviewed* in the list of alternative spellings.

   Misspellings

6. When the Speller stops on *Qnifen*, click Skip Always.

7. When the Speller stops on *mald*, double-click *mild* in the list of alternative spellings, and when the Speller stops on *repurts*, double-click *reports*.

8. When the Speller stops on the double words *the the*, click the Delete 2nd button to delete the second *the*.

   Double words

9. When the Speller stops on *PLease*, click the Replace button to correct the capitalization error.

   Incorrect capitalization

10. Finally, when the Speller stops on the proper name *Kaye*, click Skip Always.

11. When WordPerfect displays a dialog box to tell you that the spell-check is complete, click OK to close the dialog box, and then click Close in the Speller dialog box to return to the Editing screen.

The Thesaurus

You can use WordPerfect's Thesaurus to look up synonyms and antonyms for a selected word. Try this: **1.** Position the insertion point within the word you want to look up. **2.** Choose Thesaurus from the Tools menu (or press Alt-F1). The Thesaurus dialog box appears, displaying alternative words for the word you selected. These words can be either nouns (n), verbs (v), adjectives (a), or antonyms (ant). **3.** To replace the word in your document with one of these alternatives, select the new word, and click Replace. You can also select an alternative word and click Look Up to display a list of alternatives for the alternative. **4.** Click Close to close the Thesaurus dialog box. ♦

Versatile utilities

Because WordPerfect's Speller and Thesaurus are separate utilities, you don't need to be in WordPerfect to use them. In fact, you can use them in any application that is not a word-processing program. ♦

Fine-Tuning the Letter's Appearance

The letter you've typed is presentable, but you can do a few things to fine-tune its appearance. In this section, we show you how to select a base font and change margins, line spacing, and indentation.

Selecting a Base Font

The base font of a document is the font used unless you specify a different font for a particular element. Usually when you select a base font for a document, you must consider all the attributes you have used. For example, if you've used the Bold attribute, the base font you select must include bold. If you've used a size attribute such as Large or Small, the base font must be available in sizes that are larger or smaller than the base size. Because the letter you have just created doesn't include any attributes, you can select almost any available font as your base font.

Deciding which font to use

Follow these steps to select a base font for the letter:

1. Move the insertion point to the top of your document.

Changing font

2. Choose Font from the Font menu. WordPerfect displays the available fonts in the list box on the left side of this dialog box:

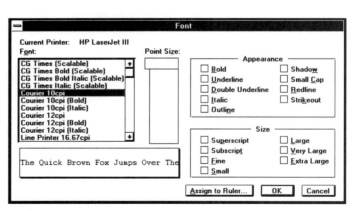

3. Move the highlight to the desired font, and double-click. You then return to the Editing screen.

4. When you select a font, WordPerfect inserts a Font code ([Font:*Font name Size*], where *Font name* is the name, and *Size* is the point size or cpi of the font you selected). Choose Reveal Codes from the View menu to see the Font code located at the top of the letter. Then choose Reveal Codes again to return to the normal Editing screen.

We selected Times as our base font, and we selected 12 as the size. Here's the result:

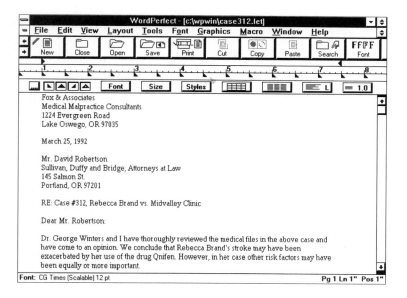

Start at the top

Move the cursor to the top of the document before you select a base font to ensure that you select a base font for the entire document. (This small but important step is easy to overlook.) ♦

Measuring up

With some printers, fixed pitch fonts, such as Courier, are measured in terms of the number of characters that print in 1 inch. The unit of measure for these fonts is designated as *characters per inch* or *cpi*. Thus a 10 cpi font prints 10 characters per inch, and a 12 cpi font prints 12 characters per inch. A 12 cpi font is therefore smaller than a 10 cpi font. ♦

Additional fonts

One source of additional fonts is Bitstream. For more information about Bitstream fonts, call (800) 522-FONT, or write to:

Bitstream Inc.
215 First Street
Cambridge, MA 02142 ♦

*Restoring the
default font*

If you change your mind about the base font you have selected and want to restore the default font, all you have to do is remove the Font code from the letter. Simply display the Reveal Codes screen by choosing Reveal Codes from the View menu, move the cursor in the Reveal Codes screen to the Font code, and press Del to delete the code.

Changing WordPerfect's Default Settings

As you work with WordPerfect, you might notice that you use the same formatting for all your documents. For example, suppose you always use the Times font. Instead of having to change the font every time you start a new document, you can change WordPerfect's default settings so that every document you create is in Times.

Let's experiment by changing the default font setting from Courier to Times:

Setting defaults

1. From the File menu, choose Preferences and then Initial Codes. WordPerfect displays this screen:

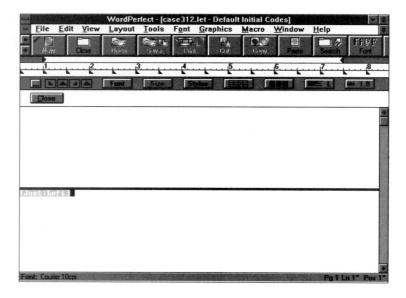

2. From the Font menu, choose Font to display the Font dialog box.
3. Double-click Times in the list box to insert a Font code, and then click the Close button to close the Initial Codes screen and return to your document.

From now on, every document you create in WordPerfect will be in Times. (The current document is already in Times; if it was formatted with a different font, that font would remain in effect for this document.) If you want to change the font of a particular document, you can still do so by positioning the insertion point at the beginning of the document, clicking the Font button, and double-clicking the desired font in the list box. Of course, you can also change the default setting back to Courier at any time.

Setting Margins

One way to balance the proportions of a letter is to change its margins. You can shorten a long letter by decreasing the margins, or lengthen a short letter by increasing the margins.

Let's add a little length to our letter, using the margin markers on the Ruler. (The margin markers are the inward-pointing arrows on either side of the Ruler. If you don't see the Ruler on your screen, choose Ruler from the View menu.) WordPerfect's default left and right margin settings are 1 inch. To change both margins for the entire letter to 1.5 inches, follow these steps:

1. Move the insertion point to the beginning of the letter. ←─────── *Increasing margins*

2. Drag the left margin marker to the 1.5-inch mark on the Ruler.

3. Now drag the right margin marker to the 7-inch mark. Here's how your screen looks now:

```
┌─────────────────────────────────────────────────────────────┐
│ ─                WordPerfect - [c:\wpwin\case312.let]      ▼ ▲│
│ ◻  File  Edit  View  Layout  Tools  Font  Graphics  Macro  Window  Help   ▲│
│ ◻ ◻   ◻   ◻    ◻    ◻    ◻    ◻    ◻    ◻  FFFF│
│   New  Close  Open  Save  Print  Cut  Copy  Paste  Search  Font│
│  ┌1┄┄┄┄2┄┄┄┄3┄┄┄┄4┄┄┄┄5┄┄┄┄6┄┄┄┄7┄┄┄┄8┐  │
│  ┌──┬─┬─┬─┬─┐ Font   Size   Styles  ▦   ▤  ≡L  = 1.0 │
│  Fox & Associates                                    ▲│
│  Medical Malpractice Consultants                      │
│  1224 Evergreen Road                                  │
│  Lake Oswego, OR 97035                                │
│                                                       │
│  March 25, 1992                                       │
│                                                       │
│  Mr. David Robertson                                  │
│  Sullivan, Duffy and Bridge, Attorneys at Law         │
│  145 Salmon St.                                       │
│  Portland, OR 97201                                   │
│                                                       │
│  RE: Case #312, Rebecca Brand vs. Midvalley Clinic    │
│                                                       │
│  Dear Mr. Robertson:                                  │
│                                                       │
│  Dr. George Winters and I have thoroughly reviewed the medical files in the │
│  above case and have come to an opinion. We conclude that Rebecca Brand's │
│  stroke may have been exacerbated by her use of the drug Qnifen. However, in │
│  her case other risk factors may have been equally or more important.   ▼│
│ Font: CG Times (Scalable) 12 pt            Pg 1 Ln 1" Pos 1.5"│
└─────────────────────────────────────────────────────────────┘
```

Notice that the text of the letter has shifted away from the left side of the screen. When you print the letter, both the left and right margins will measure 1.5 inches.

4. Click the Save button to save the letter.

The new margin settings are controlled by the Left and Right Margin code [L/R Mar:1.5",1.5"] in your document. To see this code:

1. Choose Reveal Codes from the View menu.

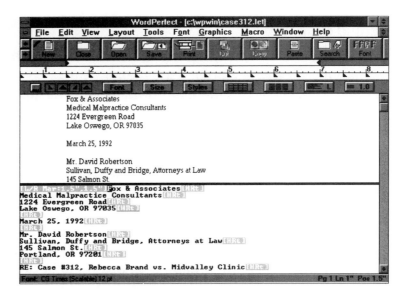

Restoring default margins

To return to the default margin setting, you can delete this code. However, leave the code in place for now.

2. Choose Reveal Codes to return to the Editing screen.

Adjusting Line Spacing

Usually, regular paragraphs in a letter are single-spaced, but sometimes you will want to change the spacing for specific elements in the letter, or you might want to specify double-spacing for drafts.

WordPerfect's default line-spacing setting is 1—single-spacing. Changing this setting to 1.5 produces one-and-a-half-spacing, and changing it to 2 produces double-spacing. These three settings are available from the Ruler. By choosing Line and then Spacing from the Layout menu, you can enter numbers like 1.8 or 2.4 for more precise control.

Follow these steps to double-space the numbered list:

1. Select the three numbered-list paragraphs and the word
    Age in the paragraph following the numbered list.
2. Point to the Spacing button on the Ruler, and hold
    down the mouse button to display the spacing options.

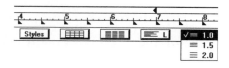

Double-spacing

3. Drag until the 2.0 option is highlighted, and then re-
    lease the mouse button. WordPerfect double-spaces
    the numbered list.
4. Choose Reveal Codes from the View menu to see the
    Line Spacing codes [Ln Spacing:2] and [Ln Spacing:1]
    that WordPerfect has inserted.
5. Choose Reveal Codes from the View menu to return
    to the Editing screen.

Indenting Paragraphs

The formatting you've added to the letter has improved the
balance of the page, but it could still use a final touch or two.
For example, we can indent the numbered list to make it stand
out. In WordPerfect, you can create several kinds of indents.
You can indent whole paragraphs; you can create hanging
indents, where the second and subsequent lines of a paragraph are indented but the first line is not; and you can indent
just the first line of a paragraph to more clearly separate it

---

Setting up a new document

When you start a new document in WordPerfect, you
can set margins, tabs, line
spacing, justification, and so
on before you begin typing.
Those settings will then
apply to the entire document,
unless you change them. ♦

Default code placement

It's important to remember
that when you add format-
ting to a document, you're
also adding codes. The formatting remains in effect
from the point in the document where its code turns it
on to the point where another
code turns it off. If you do
not select text before applying a format, by default
WordPerfect's Auto Code
Placement feature inserts the

formatting code at the beginning of the paragraph or page
containing the insertion
point. The formatting is then
applied from that point on in
the document. In some cases,
you must then turn off that
particular format by inserting another code. If you select text and apply a format,
by default WordPerfect inserts the appropriate codes at
the beginning and end of the
selection. ♦

from the preceding one. Here's a simple way to indent paragraphs:

1. Click an insertion point just before the 1 in the numbered list.

2. From the Layout menu, choose Paragraph, and then choose Indent.

3. Repeat steps 1 and 2 for the second and third paragraphs in the numbered list. This is the result:

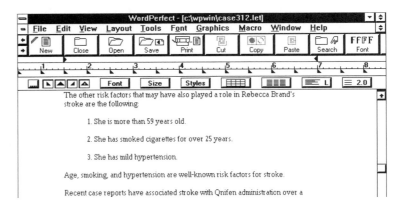

Controlling the indent →

How much you indent is a function of current tab settings. WordPerfect's default tab settings are at half-inch intervals, as indicated by the tab markers on the Ruler. You can increase or decrease these intervals using either the Ruler's tab icons or by choosing Line and Tab Set from the Layout menu. However, WordPerfect offers easy ways to accomplish tasks—such as creating tables—for which many other word-processing programs require you to set tabs, so you might never need to manipulate tabs. (We talk more about tabs in Chapter 4.)

Centering the Letter Vertically

Letters, particularly short ones, look best when they are centered on the page. By "centered," we mean that the letter is approximately the same distance from the top of the page as it is from the bottom. You could achieve this effect by adjusting your document's top and bottom margins, but using WordPerfect's Center Page feature is much easier. See for yourself:

1. With the insertion point located anywhere in the document, choose Page and Center Page from the Layout menu.

When you print the letter, it will be centered on the page.

Printing the Letter

Well, you now have an accurate, formatted letter ready for printing. When you installed WordPerfect, the setup program asked which printer you were going to use and copied to your hard drive the files necessary for WordPerfect to communicate with your printer. As we mentioned in Chapter 1, the printer we use throughout this book is a Hewlett-Packard LaserJet III. If you are using a different printer, you might have a different choice of fonts. Otherwise, you should have no difficulty printing the documents you create as you read this book.

Viewing the File

Before you print a document, you should save the file and use WordPerfect's Print Preview feature to see an overview of the document. Although you cannot edit or format text in the Print Preview screen, Print Preview is a great way to inspect your work, because you can see an entire page with

Print Preview

More about Center Page

When the Auto Code Placement feature is selected, as it is by default, WordPerfect automatically inserts the Center Page code at the beginning of the current page. However, the Center Page feature affects only the current page. If you want to vertically center multiple pages, you must choose Page and Center Page from the Layout menu for each page. ♦

Printer troubleshooting

If your printer does not print after you have made a selection from the Print menu, check that the printer is turned on and that the cable connecting the printer to your computer is securely connected at both ends. If the problem persists, check that you have selected the correct printer, by choosing Select Printer from the File menu. If you don't see your printer listed in the Available Printers list box, you can add it by clicking the Add button and then double-clicking the correct printer in the Add Printer dialog box. Be aware that you also have to copy the printer's description files to the WordPerfect program directory (C:\WPC). ♦

all the elements in place, just as they will be when printed. Here's how to view a document:

1. From the File menu, choose Print Preview to display this representation of your letter in the Print Preview screen:

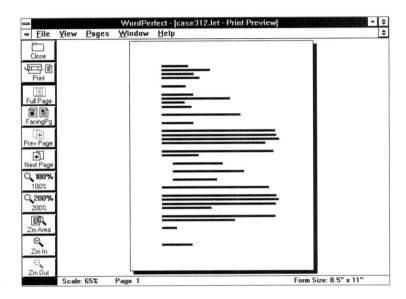

*Print Preview
Button Bar*

2. To get a better look, click 100% on the Print Preview Button Bar. Click 200% to magnify the document. You can also click Zm In repeatedly to get a progressively closer view of the page, or click Zm Out repeatedly to get a progressively broader view of the page. Click Zm Area and drag the mouse pointer over a section of the page to get a close-up view of that area. (The FacingPg, Prev Page, and Next Page buttons are for use with multipage documents.)
3. To redisplay the entire document, click Full Page.

Sending the File to the Printer

*Printing from
Print Preview*

Now for the real test. After you view the letter, printing it is a three-step process:

1. Click the Print button on the Print Preview Button Bar. WordPerfect displays this dialog box:

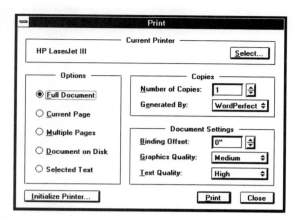

2. Check that the Full Document option is selected. If it isn't, click it to select the option.

3. Click the Print button. While WordPerfect sends the file to the printer, it displays the Current Print Job dialog box to report its progress.

4. When printing is complete, save the letter again. The printed letter looks similar to this one:

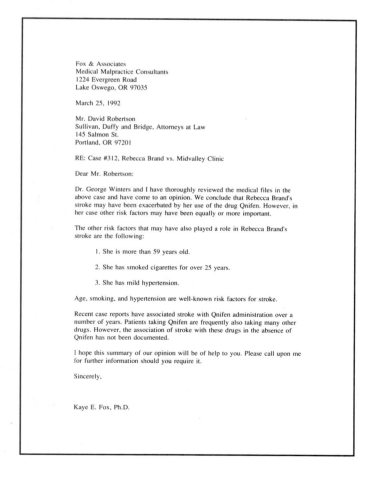

3

Great-Looking Letterheads

Applying several attributes
Page 59

Center justification
Page 55

Thin lines
Page 70

Thick gray lines
Page 70

Opening a document from File Manager
Page 65

File Manager
Page 63

Moving files
Page 75

F & A Associates
Medical Malpractice Consultants
1224 Evergreen Road
Lake Oswego, OR 97035

March 25, 1992

Mr. David Robertson
Sullivan, Duffy and Bridge, Attorneys at Law
145 Salmon St.
Portland, OR 97201

RE: Case #312, Rebecca Brand vs. Midv

Dear Mr. Robertson:

Dr. George Winters and I have thorough
have come to an opinion. We conclude t
exacerbated by her use of the drug Qnife
been equally or more important.

The other risk factors that may have also
following:

    1. She is more than 59 years old.

    2. She has smoked cigarettes for

    3. She has mild hypertension.

Age, smoking, and hypertension are well

Recent case reports have associated strok
Patients taking Qnifen are frequently also
of stroke with these drugs in the absence

I hope this summary of our opinion will
information should you require it.

Sincerely,

Kaye

Fox & Associates
==
1224 Evergreen Road   **Lake Oswego, OR 97035**   **(503) 555-4567**

March 25, 1992

Mr. David Robertson
Sullivan, Duffy and Bridge, Attorneys at Law
145 Salmon St.
Portland, OR 97201

RE: Case #312, Rebecca Brand vs. Midvalley Clinic

Dear Mr. Robertson:

Dr. George Winters and I have thoroughly reviewed the medical files in the above case and
have come to an opinion. We conclude that Rebecca Brand's stroke may have been
exacerbated by her use of the drug Qnifen. However, in her case other risk factors may have
been equally or more important.

The other risk factors that may have also played a role in Rebecca Brand's stroke are the
following:

    1. She is more than 59 years old.

WordPerfect File Manager

File Edit Search View Info Applications Window Help

| Open | Copy | Move | Delete | Find Word | Find Files | File List | Quick List | Edit QL |

Navigator - c:\wpwin

Drives	c:\	wpwin	
[-a-]	[wpwin]	[graphics]	
[-c-]	autoexec.bat	[learn]	
[-d-]	autoexec.dos	[macros]	
	autoexec.old	[wp]wp{td.1]	
	autoexec.win	case312.bk!	
	bdos.bat	case312.let	
	boot.com	install.exe	
	boot.sys	install.ico	

Viewer - c:\wpwin\case312.let

Fox & Associates
Medical Malpractice Consultants
1224 Evergreen Road
Lake Oswego, OR 97035

March 25, 1992

Mr. David Robertson
Sullivan, Duffy and Bridge, Attorneys at Law

3,627,763 bytes in 32 files, 530,432 bytes free

ver a number of years.
ever, the association

pon me for further

In Chapter 1 you learned how to change the appearance of individual characters and words, and in Chapter 2 you learned how to change the look of whole paragraphs. In this chapter, we'll show you how to combine these formatting capabilities to create a couple of letterheads.

Most businesses use letterhead stationery. The advantage of using a computer-generated letterhead is that you don't have to switch the paper in your printer from plain bond to letterhead every time you print a letter. If you work for a company that already has preprinted letterhead, you probably have no choice about using it. However, you might want to use the instructions in this chapter to create a letterhead for your personal correspondence. As you follow along, you will probably think of other ways you can put the letterhead techniques to work—generating eye-catching advertisements or attractive flyers, for example.

A Simple Letterhead

First, we'll show you how to create the simple centered letterhead shown on the previous page. This letterhead is easy to generate and is a good way to become familiar with the various features WordPerfect provides for creating display type—a fancy term for words that are intended to catch the eye.

Well, let's begin. If you're at the C> prompt, type *win wpwin* to start the WordPerfect program. Then, with a clear screen in front of you, follow these steps:

1. To center the words you are going to type, select the Center option from the Justification list on the Ruler. The insertion point jumps to the middle of the window.

2. Type the text of the letterhead. For example, we entered the four lines shown at the top of the next page, pressing Enter to end each line.

3. Press Enter three more times after the last line, to create a buffer space between the letterhead and the text of any memo or letter you type.

4. Insert a [Just:Left] code so that any text following the letterhead is left-justified rather than center-justified. With the insertion point at the end of the letterhead, select Left from the Justification list on the Ruler.

Speedy Formatting

Now let's format the letterhead. Looking back at the illustration at the beginning of the chapter, you'll see that the entire letterhead is in the Times font, and it is also italic with key letters in large bold type. We don't have to select the font because in Chapter 2 we changed the default base font for all new documents to 12-point Times (see page 48). If you chose a different font because Times is not available with your printer, keep in mind that your letterhead might look a bit different from ours.

Follow these steps to apply the Italic and Fine attributes, which affect the majority of the text:

1. Select all four lines of the letterhead.

2. Click the Font button on the Button Bar. WordPerfect displays the Font dialog box:

Applying several attributes

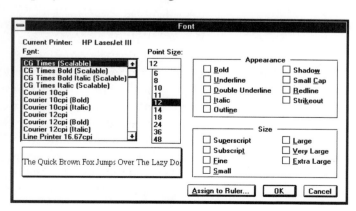

3. Select Italic from the Appearance section and Fine from the Size section. The sample text in the dialog box shows you the effects of your selections.

4. Click OK to confirm your selections and close the dialog box. Then click anywhere to remove the highlighting from the lines, as shown here:

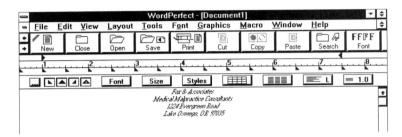

Now let's tackle the characters we want to emphasize. In the example letterhead, we want the *F* in *Fox*, the ampersand (&), and the *A* in *Associates* to be both bold and bigger. Follow along with the appropriate letters in your letterhead:

1. Drag across the *F* in *Fox* to select it. (If you find it difficult to select a single italic character with the mouse, click an insertion point in front of the *F*, hold down the Shift key, and press the Right Arrow key.)

2. Click the Font button. In the Font dialog box, select Bold from the Appearance section and Very Large from the Size section, and then click OK.

3. Repeat the previous steps for the *A* in *Associates*.

Finding fonts quickly

If the Font list box displays many fonts, type the first letter of the font you're looking for. The highlight instantly moves to the first font name that begins with that letter. If you type the next letter of the font name, the highlight moves to the first font name that matches the two letters you've typed, and so on. ♦

Size attributes

WordPerfect calculates the settings for the size attributes—Fine, Small, Large, Very Large, Extra Large, Superscript, and Subscript—as percentages of the currently selected font. You can change these percentages in the Print Settings dialog box, which you access by choosing Preferences and then Print from the File menu. ♦

Templates

Templates contain basic information and formatting that you use repeatedly. The letterhead is a good candidate for a template, as is the memo you created in Chapter 1. After saving a template, all you have to do to use it is open the template file, save it with a new name to preserve the file intact for future use, and then use it as the basis for the current letter or memo. ♦

4.   Repeat the same steps for the ampersand (&), selecting Large in step 2 instead of Very Large.

Before you go any further, save the letterhead:

1.   Click the Save button on the Button Bar.

2.   In the Save As dialog box, type *lh1.tem* (for Letterhead 1 Template) in the Save As edit box, and click Save.

We recommend that you always use the filename extension TEM for files that you want to use as templates (see page 60). The extension will remind you to save any documents created with the letterhead template under a different name, so that you can preserve the template intact for future use.

Saving documents as templates

Test Printing

The next step is to print a test copy of the letterhead so that we can determine what adjustments we need to make, if any.

1.   Click the Print button on the Button Bar.

2.   Check that Full Document is selected, and click Print.

Take a moment to admire your efforts, which look something like the letterhead shown here:

*F*ox *& A*ssociates

Medical Malpractice Consultants
1224 Evergreen Road
Lake Oswego, OR 97035

Fine-Tuning

Take a good look at the printed letterhead shown above. Notice the space between the *F* and the *o* in *Fox*. The other letters are evenly spaced, but the *F* and the *o* seem too far apart. Inconsistencies in letter spacing are the result of differences in the shapes and slants of various letters. You can manually decrease or increase the amount of space between letters by using WordPerfect's Kerning feature. As you might have guessed, adjusting the space between letters is called *kerning*. Let's kern the *F* and the *o* in *Fox*.

Kerning

1.   Click an insertion point to the left of the *o* in *Fox*.

2. Choose Typesetting from the Layout menu. In the Typesetting dialog box, click the Manual Kerning button to display this dialog box:

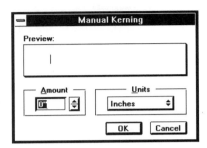

3. Click the down arrow in the Amount section until -0.027" is displayed. You can see the effect of your kerning in the Preview box of the Manual Kerning dialog box.
4. Click OK twice to return to the Editing screen.

WordPerfect has decreased the space between the *F* and the *o* in *Fox* by 27/1000s of an inch. (To increase the space between two letters, simply enter a positive number.)

Inserting the Date

Before we move on to the next section, let's add a Date code to the letterhead so that WordPerfect will automatically insert the current date (based on your computer's system clock) each time you open the letterhead. Here's how:

Adding a Date code

1. Press PgDn to move the insertion point to the end of the letterhead.
2. From the Tools menu, choose Date and then Code. WordPerfect inserts the current date in your document. (You can display the Reveal Codes screen to see the Date code.) Here's how the letterhead looks now:

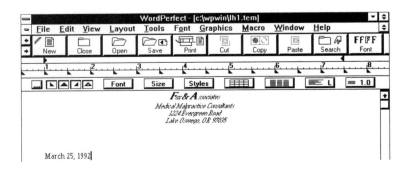

If you want to change the format of the date, you can do so by choosing Preferences and Date Format from the File menu, and then editing the format in the Date/Time Preferences dialog box. (Use the Predefined Dates or Date Codes drop-down list boxes to edit the current date format.)

Changing the date format

Now you're ready to save the letterhead and clear the Editing screen:

1. Click the Close button on the Button Bar. WordPerfect displays a dialog box asking whether you want to save changes to the document.

2. Click Yes. WordPerfect saves the document with the name you assigned earlier, and clears the screen.

Locating Documents

One way to add the letterhead to a business document is to open the letterhead template, save the open letterhead with a new name to avoid overwriting the template, and then create the document below the letterhead. Another way is to work on a draft of your document, finalize its content and formatting, and then merge the letterhead at the top. In the latter case, you need a quick way of finding and retrieving the letterhead template, and nothing could be quicker and easier than WordPerfect's File Manager. You can use File Manager to:

File Manager

- Find files, based on their names or by searching through their text.
- View a file's contents without actually opening the file.
- Copy, delete, move, open, and print files.
- Create new directories.

Let's look at a simple example of how you might put File Manager to use. Suppose you have just started a new Word-Perfect session and you want to retrieve the letter you wrote in the previous chapter and then merge the letterhead you just created at the top. Follow these steps to locate the letter with File Manager:

1. Choose File Manager from the File menu. When File Manager is loaded, you see the screen on the next page.

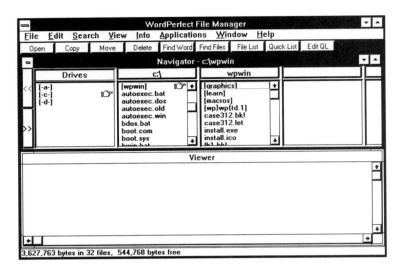

File Manager enables you to look at information about your files from several viewpoints. By default, File Manager displays its Navigator and Viewer windows. You can also display the File List and Quick List windows by choosing Layouts from the View menu, and then selecting the combination of windows you want.

Other views →

2. In the WPWIN list box, click the CASE312.LET file-name to highlight it, and notice that the text of the letter is now visible in the Viewer window:

Drives and directories in File Manager

Because you opened File Manager from a Word-Perfect document located in the C:\WPWIN directory, the directories on your C:\ drive and the files in the C:\WPWIN directory are already displayed in their respective list boxes in the Navigator window. To display the files on other drives or in other directories, in the Navigator window simply double-click the name of the drive or directory you want. WordPerfect then displays the contents of the drive or directory you selected in the adjacent list box. ♦

The File List and Quick List windows

Click the File List button on the File Manager Button Bar to see a list of subdirectories and files in the current directory. The list includes the size of each file (in kilobytes) and the date and time the files were last saved. You can also access and edit the Quick List from File Manager by clicking the Quick List and Edit QL buttons, respectively. ♦

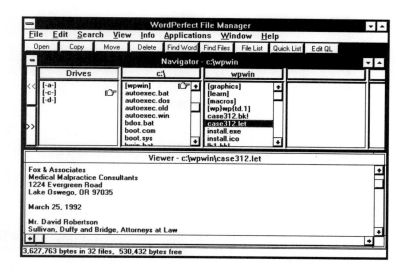

3. Click the Open button on the Button Bar, and then click the Open button in the Open dialog box. File Manager closes and the letter is now open on your screen.

Opening a document from File Manager

Well, that was easy. This demonstration has probably given you a feel for how useful File Manager will be once your hard disk is crowded with documents. With File Manager, you no longer have to rely on cryptic eight-character filenames to jog your memory about a file's contents. You might want to explore File Manager further, perhaps browsing through the Help file to get some idea of the scope of this powerful utility. But for now, let's move on.

Help with File Manager

Merging the Letterhead into the Letter

Now that you have the letter open on your screen, you're ready to merge in the letterhead. Here's how:

1. Press Ctrl-Home to move the insertion point to the beginning of the document.
2. Choose Retrieve from the File menu. WordPerfect displays the Retrieve File dialog box.

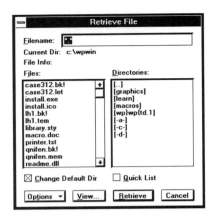

3. Select LH1.TEM from the Files list box, and click Retrieve.

4. When WordPerfect asks whether to insert the file in the current document, click Yes to merge the letterhead at the top of the letter, as shown here:

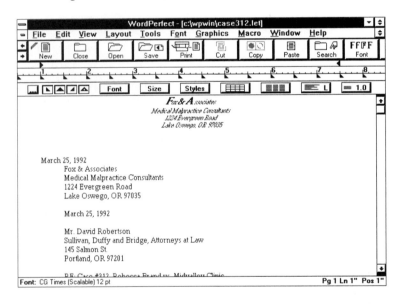

Filename after merging →

After the merge, notice the filename in the title bar at the top of the document window. The merged document retains the filename CASE312.LET, because the letterhead was retrieved into the letter. (If the letter had been retrieved into the letterhead, the filename would be LH1.TEM.)

More Fine-Tuning

As you can see, the merged document needs a little cosmetic surgery before we print it.

1. First, delete the second return address and date—not the Date code—because the letterhead now supplies that information. Simply select the address and date, and press the Del key.

2. Next, align the letter with the letterhead by restoring its default margins. In the Reveal Codes screen, move the cursor to the [L/R Mar:1.5",1.5"] code, and press Del. The margins of the letter instantly return to 1 inch.

3. Choose Save As from the File menu, type a different filename—perhaps, *case312.lh1*—so that you can use the unmerged letter later in the chapter, and click the Save button.

Now let's print the merged letter:

1. Click the Print button on the Button Bar.

2. Check that Full Document is selected, and click the Print button.

3. Click the Close button to close CASE312.LH1 and clear the screen in preparation for the next letterhead.

There's more than one way

In the example above, you could have just as easily aligned the letterhead with the letter by placing the insertion point at the beginning of the letterhead and increasing its left and right margins to 1.5 inches. ♦

Printing selected pages

If the file you are printing has multiple pages, you can select any or all of the pages to be printed. After clicking the Print button on the Button Bar to display the Print dialog box, here's what you do: 1. Select Multiple Pages from the Options section. 2. Click the Print button at the bottom of the dialog box. 3. In the Multiple Pages dialog box, specify in the Range text box the pages you want to print, as follows: If you enter 3,5 or 3 5, pages 3 and 5 are printed; if you enter 3-5, pages 3, 4, and 5 are printed; and if you enter 3,5,7-10, pages 3, 5, and 7 through 10 are printed. 4. Click Print to proceed. ♦

A More Sophisticated Letterhead

The letterhead you just created does the job, but it's very simple. Let's now explore some of the WordPerfect features that can help you create a more sophisticated letterhead. As you follow along, refer to the other letterhead pictured at the beginning of the chapter, so you can see the effect you are aiming for. Again, you can use the example name and address or substitute your own. We're going to work on this letterhead one section at a time, entering and formatting the name and address first and then dressing them up with lines. As with the previous letterhead, we don't have to worry about the font and size of the document because they are predefined as 12-point Times by the initial codes we set in Chapter 2. We can therefore focus on the rest of the formats:

1. Choose Bold from the Font menu to turn on the Bold attribute, type *Fox & Associates*, and then press Enter twice to add some space.

2. To make the name both bold and italic, let's add the Italic attribute. Point to the name, triple-click to select it, click the Font button on the Button Bar, and in the Font dialog box, select Italic from the Appearance section.

3. Select Very Large from the Size section, and click OK. Here's the result so far:

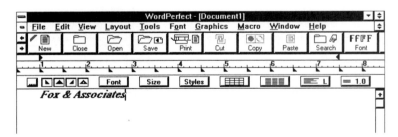

The address in the example letterhead is fairly long, and we want to make it bold but small so that it will fit on a single line. Follow these steps to create an address line like the one shown on page 57.

1. Press PgDn to move to the end of the document, click the Font button, select Bold in the Appearance section, and select Small in the Size section. Click OK.

2. Type *1224 Evergreen Road.*

3. From the Layout menu, choose Line and then Center. The insertion point moves to the center of the screen.

    Moving to the center

4. Type *Lake Oswego, OR 97035.*

5. With the insertion point at the end of the address, choose Line and then Flush Right from the Layout menu. The insertion point moves to the right edge of the screen.

    Moving to the right

6. Type *(503) 555-4567.* Notice how the characters move backward as you type. Using WordPerfect's Flush Right feature ensures that the telephone number is aligned with the right margin.

That's it for the text of the letterhead. Now let's dress it up a bit.

Adding Lines

You've created a functional but plain letterhead. In this section, we show you how to use WordPerfect's Graphics feature to draw two kinds of lines between the name and the address: a thin, solid black line and a somewhat thicker, gray line. When you are familiar with basic line-drawing techniques, you can experiment on your own, adding different lines and boxes to create the effect you want. For now, follow these steps:

1. Click an insertion point on the blank line below the name line.

2. To draw the first line, choose Line from the Graphics menu, and then choose Horizontal. WordPerfect displays this dialog box:

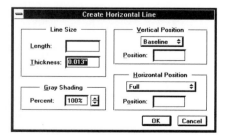

As you can see, the Thickness text box, which is highlighted, shows a default line thickness of 0.013 inch.

Thin lines →

3. Type *.02*.
4. Click the arrows in the Vertical Position section, and then select the Specify option. In the Position text box, type *1.25* to position the first line 1.25 inches from the top of the page.
5. The other settings in the dialog box are as you want them, so click OK to return to the Editing screen.

Now for the next line:

1. Be sure the insertion point is located just below the first horizontal line. (Open the Reveal Codes screen, and check that the cursor is resting on the Hard Return code after the Horizontal Line code.)
2. From the Graphics menu, again choose Line and then Horizontal.

Thick gray lines →

3. Type *.05* in the Thickness text box.
4. To make the line gray instead of black, click the downward-pointing arrow to the right of the Percent box in the Gray Shading section until the text box shows a setting of 70%. (A setting of 70% means that the line is 70 percent black dots and 30 percent white dots, which creates a dark gray.) If 70% scrolls by too quickly, click the upward-pointing arrow to back up.
5. Select Specify in the Vertical Position section, and type *1.35* in the Position text box.

Vertical lines

You can draw vertical lines in your documents as well as horizontal ones. Follow these steps: **1.** From the Graphics menu, choose Line and then Vertical. **2.** In the Create Vertical Line dialog box, specify the line's size, position, and shading. **3.** Then click OK. ♦

Editing lines

To edit a horizontal or vertical line in your document: **1.** Choose Line and then Edit Horizontal or Edit Vertical from the Graphics menu. WordPerfect selects the appropriate line and then displays the Edit Horizontal Line or Edit Vertical Line dialog box. **2.** Make the necessary changes, and click OK to return to the Editing screen. ♦

Repositioning lines

In addition to specifying horizontal and vertical line positions in the Edit Horizontal and Edit Vertical Line dialog boxes, you can reposition a line in your document by simply clicking the line with your mouse pointer to select it and then dragging the line to a new location. ♦

6. Click OK to return to the Editing screen.

7. Save this letterhead with the name *lh2.tem*.

Test Printing

As with the first letterhead you created, the next step is to print a test copy of the file to be sure that all your formatting is in place and that the lines are positioned correctly. Follow these steps:

1. Click the Print button on the Button Bar to display the Print dialog box.

2. Check that Full Document is selected, and click Print.

The printed letterhead looks something like this:

A Final Touch

This letterhead shaped up fairly well, but why don't we add a Date code here, as we did for the previous letterhead:

Adding graphics

In Chapter 5, we show you how to import graphics into your WordPerfect documents. Graphics can greatly increase the impact of your letterhead. WordPerfect for Windows comes with a set of ready-made graphics files that you can work with, or you can create graphics of your own in a drawing or paint program. As long as the file is saved in a format that WordPerfect supports, you can import it with ease. Then it's simple to size and crop the graphic until it is small enough to use as a design element in your letterhead. See page 114 for information about importing procedures, and page 77 for examples of letterheads that incorporate graphics. ◆

The Line Draw feature

In addition to using commands on the Graphics menu to draw lines, you can also use WordPerfect's Line Draw feature, which lets you create lines and boxes with a variety of preset characters. Simply press Ctrl-D to display the Line Draw dialog box, select the character you want, and use the Arrow keys to draw your lines. ◆

1. Press Ctrl-End to move the insertion point to the end of the letterhead, and then press Enter four times to create some space between the letterhead and the date.

2. Now add the Date code at the insertion point by choosing Date and then Code from the Tools menu. The letter head now looks like this:

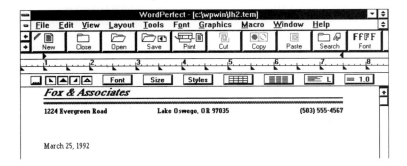

3. Before you move on, click the Save button on the Button Bar to save the letterhead.

Merging the Letter into the Letterhead

Now we can merge the letterhead with the example letter. This time, we'll copy the letter from its document window and paste it into the letterhead document window. With the example letterhead still displayed on your screen, follow these steps:

1. Load File Manager by choosing File Manager from the File menu. Use the Navigator to find the CASE312.LET file, and then open the file as described on page 65.

2. Click an insertion point just before the *M* in *Mr. David Robertson*. (You don't need to select the return address or date, because they're already included in the letterhead.) Scroll to the bottom of the letter using the scroll box on the left side of the document window. Now point to the end of the letter (just after *Ph.D.*), hold down the Shift key, and then click the mouse button to select the letter.

3. To copy the selected text, click the Copy button on the Button Bar.

4. Choose Tile from the Window menu. WordPerfect divides the screen in two and displays the letter's window in the top half and the letterhead's window in the bottom half.

Splitting the screen

5. Click the letterhead's window to make it active, and then press Ctrl-End to position the insertion point at the end of the document, after all the codes.

6. Press Enter twice to add some space below the date in the letterhead. Then click the Paste button to place the copy of the letter beneath the letterhead.

Pasting text from another document

7. Now view the merged document in the Print Preview screen. Here's what you see:

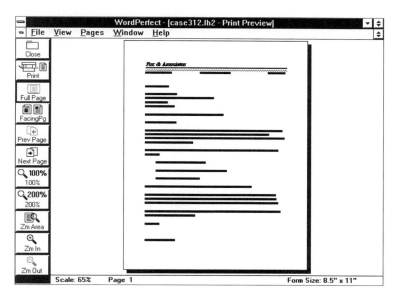

You don't have to worry about adjusting the margins of the letter this time, because the [L\R Mar:1.5",1.5"] code was not included in the text you copied and pasted into the letterhead document.

8. Click Close to return to the Editing screen, and save the merged document with an appropriate name, such as *case312.lh2*.

Now close CASE312.LET by following these steps:

1. Click the CASE312.LET window to activate it, and then click the Close button on the Button Bar.

Closing the second window

Expanding the window

2. Now click the CASE312.LH2 window's Maximize button (the upward-pointing arrow in the top-right corner) to expand the document window to full size.
3. Print the document by clicking the Print button on the Button Bar, checking the settings in the Print dialog box, and clicking Print. The result should be identical to the letter at the beginning of the chapter.
4. Click the Close button to close CASE312.LH2.

Moving the Letterheads to Their Own Directory

If you couldn't resist exploring File Manager earlier in the chapter, you'll know that you can do a lot more with File Manager than simply locate files. In this section, we'll show you how you can use File Manager to organize your WordPerfect documents without having to leave WordPerfect. We'll create a directory called *LET_HEAD* and then move the two letterhead files from the current directory (WPWIN) into the new directory.

Follow these steps to create the directory:

Creating a new directory

1. First, load File Manager by choosing File Manager from the File menu.
2. Next, choose Create Directory from the File menu. File Manager displays this dialog box:

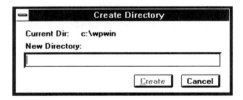

3. In the New Directory text box, type *let_head*, and then click Create. File Manager closes the dialog box and redisplays the Navigator window with the new LET_HEAD directory added to its WPWIN list box.

Now let's move the letterhead files:

Finding files

1. Choose Find Files from the Search menu. File Manager displays this dialog box:

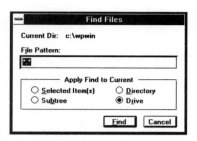

2. In the File Pattern text box, replace *.* (which means "all the files, no matter what their filenames and extensions") with *.*tem* (which means "all the files that have the extension TEM, no matter what their filenames").

Specifying files with wildcards

3. Click the Directory option to search for the files only in the current directory (WPWIN), and then click the Find button. File Manager displays the Performing Search box to tell you that it's hard at work, and then displays this report of its search results:

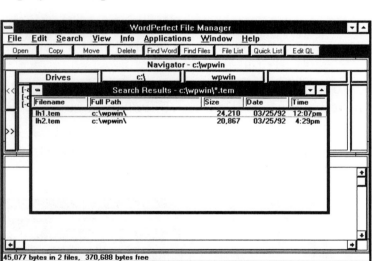

As you can see, File Manager has located the two letterhead files.

4. Choose Select All from the Edit menu.

5. Choose Move/Rename from the File menu. File Manager displays the Move/Rename File(s) dialog box.

Moving files

6. In the To Directory text box, click an insertion point after the *n* in c:\wpwin, type *let_head*, and then click Move All. File Manager reports its progress as it moves the files.

7. Close the Search Results dialog box (which is now empty) by double-clicking the Control menu box at the left end of its title bar.

To be sure the LH1.TEM and LH2.TEM files really were moved to the new directory, follow these steps:

1. In the WPWIN list box, double-click LET_HEAD to display its files in the empty list box to the right. Here's what you see:

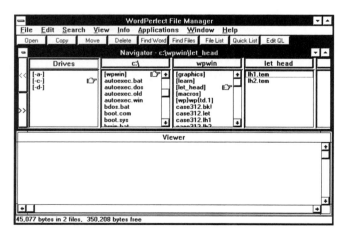

Quitting File Manager →

2. Knowing that the letterheads are safely stored in their own directory, quit the File Manager by choosing Exit from the File menu.

That's all there is to it. Now you can create directories to organize all your WordPerfect documents.

Below, you see a few other examples of letterheads that you can create in WordPerfect for Windows. By the time you finish reading this book, you should be able to figure out for yourself how to duplicate these examples or generate your own snazzy letterhead.

We've now covered the information you need to know to create two common types of business documents: memos and letters. In the next chapter, we show you how to create the elements often included in reports.

4

Professional Reports

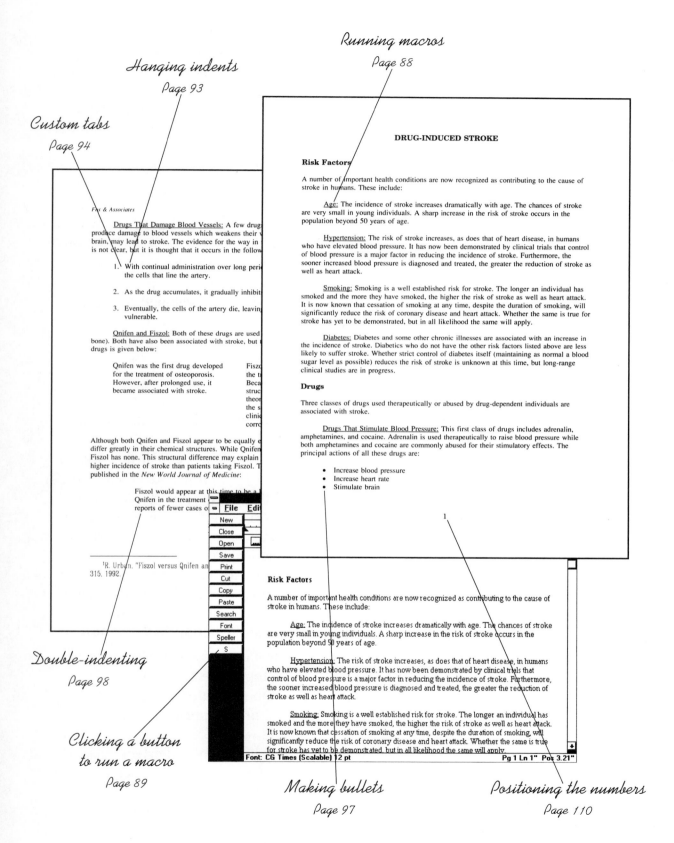

Custom tabs — Page 94

Hanging indents — Page 93

Running macros — Page 88

Double-indenting — Page 98

Clicking a button to run a macro — Page 89

Making bullets — Page 97

Positioning the numbers — Page 110

In many professions, writing reports is a daily task. Whether you're a scientist, an administrative assistant, a marketing specialist, or an attorney, WordPerfect for Windows can help take the drudgery out of report writing. In this chapter, we'll introduce you to WordPerfect features for creating outlines, lists, footnotes, and parallel columns. In addition, we'll show you how to create simple macros and how to add headers and numbers to your pages.

To demonstrate all these features, we need to work with a document that is longer than those we created in previous chapters. You can either create a report of your own or you can use the one shown on the previous page. As you follow along, you type just enough text to use the feature we are discussing. You can refer to the figures on the previous page to see how all these features can be combined to create a useful report.

Outlining a Document

Different people work in different ways. Some people launch right into a project, starting at the beginning and working their way through in a linear fashion until they've crossed the last *t* and dotted the last *i*. Others depend heavily on outlines, creating an overview of the project and then filling in the details. If you fall into the latter category, this section is for you. Although the report we're writing is relatively short, it contains enough headings to give you a good idea of how WordPerfect's Outline feature works.

The Outline feature allows you to create up to eight levels of headings, each with a unique identification scheme, known collectively as paragraph numbers. Follow these steps to see how easy it is to create an outline in WordPerfect:

1. Start with a clear WordPerfect screen. (Be sure the insertion point is at the top of the screen.)

Creating an outline

2. From the Tools menu, choose Outline, and then choose Outline On. The word *Outline* appears in the bottom-left corner of the screen.

3. Press Enter to start the outline. WordPerfect inserts a Roman numeral I at the top of the Editing screen.

4. Choose Reveal Codes from the View menu. In the Reveal Codes screen, notice that WordPerfect has

inserted an Outline On code ([Outline On]) and Paragraph Number code ([Par Num:Auto]). Every time you press Enter while Outline is turned on, WordPerfect inserts a Paragraph Number code after the hard return to designate a new outline level. Choose Reveal Codes again to turn off the Reveal Codes screen.

Now enter the headings of the outline, using the Backspace or Del key if you make a mistake:

1. From the Layout menu, choose Paragraph and then Indent to indent the text you'll type after I. (Don't press the Tab key which, as you'll see in a minute, is used to change the outline level.)

2. Press the Caps Lock key, then type *DRUG-INDUCED STROKE*, and press Enter to start a new heading. WordPerfect inserts II at the beginning of the line. Press Caps Lock again to turn off capitalization.

3. Press the Tab key to change this heading to level two. The insertion point moves over one tab, and A replaces II. Press F7 (the keyboard shortcut for the Indent command), type *Drugs*, and press Enter to start a new line. WordPerfect inserts B at the beginning of the line.

Changing outline levels

4. Press Tab to change to level three. The insertion point moves over one more tab, and 1 replaces B.

5. Press F7, type *Drugs That Stimulate Blood Pressure*, and press Enter to start a new line. WordPerfect inserts 2 at the beginning of the line.

6. Repeat the previous step for the headings *Drugs That Damage Blood Vessels* and *Qnifen and Fiszol*. (Be sure to press Enter after each heading.)

7. Press Shift-Tab to change from level three to level two. The insertion point moves back one tab, and the paragraph number B replaces 4. Press F7, type *Risk Factors*, and press Enter to start a new line.

8. Press Tab to change to level three.

9. Again press F7, type *Age*, and press Enter to start a new line.

10. Repeat the previous step for the headings *Hypertension* and *Smoking*. The results are on the next page.

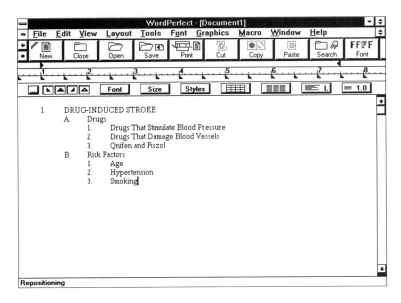

Now turn off Outline mode:

1. Without moving the insertion point from the end of the *Smoking* heading, choose Outline and Outline Off from the Tools menu.

2. Choose Reveal Codes from the View menu. Notice the codes WordPerfect has inserted, including the Outline Off code at the end of the document. Choose Reveal Codes again to turn off the Reveal Codes screen.

Reviewing the outline, you decide that the risk-factors discussion should precede the drugs discussion. Word-Perfect makes it easy to quickly take care of this kind of outline reorganization by treating main headings and their subordinate headings as a "family." Follow these steps to move the *Risk Factors* family above the *Drugs* family:

Reorganizing the outline

1. Click an insertion point anywhere in the *Risk Factors* heading, and choose Outline and then Move Family from the Tools menu. WordPerfect highlights the entire family.

2. Press the Up Arrow key once so that the *Risk Factors* family is located above the *Drugs* family, and press Enter to confirm the new location. WordPerfect renumbers the headings to reflect their revised order.

Now suppose you want to add a level-three heading under *Smoking*. Here's what you do:

1. Click an insertion point at the end of the *Smoking* heading, and press Enter.

Adding headings

2. Press F7 to create an indent, and type *Diabetes*. Here's how the outline looks now:

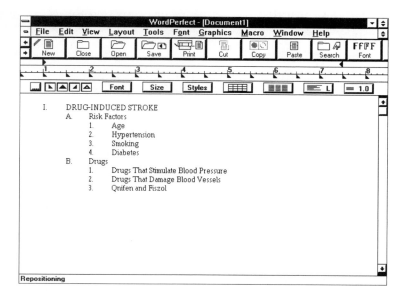

3. All that's left to do is save the outline. Click the Save button on the Button Bar, and save the outline with the filename *stroke.rpt*.

Changing numbering style

To change the numbering style used in the outline: **1.** From the Tools menu, choose Outline and Define. **2.** In the Define Paragraph Numbering dialog box, display the Predefined Formats drop-down list box, and select the style you want. **3.** Click OK to return to the Editing screen.

If you're changing the style of an existing outline, you must be sure the insertion point is at the beginning of the outline before you choose Outline and Define from the Tools menu. ♦

Changing levels

To change the level of an existing outline heading, in the Reveal Codes screen place the cursor to the right of the Paragraph Number code of the heading you want to change, and then press Tab (for the next level) or Shift-Tab (for the previous level). ♦

Filling In the Outline

You can use the outline you just created as a starting point for the actual report. All you have to do is remove the Outline On and Off codes and the Hard Tab and Paragraph Number codes, which will give you a chance to use the Search and Replace features discussed in Chapter 2. To remove the codes, follow these steps:

1. Choose Reveal Codes from the View menu, move the cursor in the Reveal Codes screen to the Outline On code, and then press the Del key. WordPerfect simultaneously deletes the Outline Off code.

2. Next, delete the Hard Return code ([HRt]) at the top of the outline.

3. Now let's delete the Hard Tab codes. With the Reveal Codes screen still displayed, choose Replace from the Edit menu. In the Search And Replace dialog box, click Codes. WordPerfect displays this dialog box:

Using Replace to delete codes

4. Scroll down to the [HdTab] code in the Search Codes list box, and click Insert to enter the code in the Search For text box. Leave the Replace With text box empty so that WordPerfect replaces the Hard Tab codes with nothing, and click Replace All. When WordPerfect has deleted the Hard Tab codes from the outline, click Close to close the Search And Replace dialog box. All the headings change to level one.

5. Next, replace the Paragraph Number codes with nothing. Press Ctrl-Home, choose Replace from the Edit menu, and click Codes. Now type *par* to scroll the Search Codes list box to the Par Num code, double-click the code to insert it in the Search For text box,

and then click Replace All. When WordPerfect has deleted the Par Num codes from the outline, click Close to close the Search And Replace dialog box.

6. Now for the Indent codes, some of which you want to delete and some of which you want to replace with tabs. Press Ctrl-Home, and delete the Indent code preceding the *DRUG-INDUCED STROKE* heading. Then delete the Indent codes preceding the *Risk Factors* and *Drugs* headings.

7. To replace the remaining Indent codes with tabs, again press Ctrl-Home. Choose Replace from the Edit menu, click the Codes button, type i to move to Indent in the list box, and double-click to insert the code in the Search For text box. Next, click the Replace With text box, click Codes, type *Tab*, and click Insert. Click Replace All, and when WordPerfect has made the replacements, click Close to close the Search And Replace dialog box.

8. Choose Reveal Codes from the View menu to return to the Editing screen.

9. Click the Save button to save the report headings, which look like this:

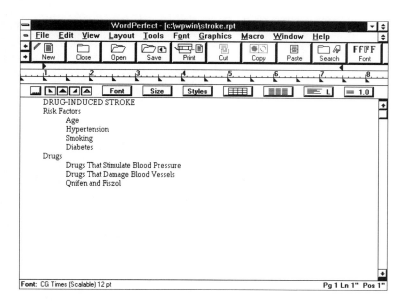

Now you're ready to start entering and formatting the text of the report.

1. Triple-click the *DRUG-INDUCED STROKE* heading, and then select Center from the Ruler's Justification list to center the heading.
2. With the heading still selected, choose Bold from the Font menu to make the heading bold. Press End and then press Enter twice to add two blank lines between this heading and the next one.
3. Triple-click the *Risk Factors* heading, and repeat the previous step.
4. With the insertion point at the beginning of the second blank line after *Risk Factors*, type the following:

   A number of important health conditions are now recognized as contributing to the cause of stroke in humans. These include:

5. Press Enter once to add a blank line below the text.
6. Triple-click the *Drugs* heading, and repeat step 2.
7. With the insertion point at the beginning of the second blank line after *Drugs*, type the following:

   Three classes of drugs used therapeutically or abused by drug-dependent individuals are associated with stroke.

8. Press Enter once to add a blank line.
9. Now type a colon after each of the seven level-three headings.
10. Finally, click the Save button to save the *STROKE.RPT* document.

Automating Tasks with Macros

In the course of carrying out your work, you will often find yourself repeating the same task over and over again. For example, you might have to repeatedly type the same name or phrase, or you might need to format a series of headings with the same attributes. For times like these, WordPerfect's Macro feature comes in handy.

WordPerfect macros are scripts, or small programs, that automate tasks normally accomplished with a series of key-strokes. You can create macros that perform all sorts of tasks—from saving and printing a file to typing a letterhead.

You simply give the macro a name, "record" the keystrokes that you want the macro to duplicate, and then "play back" the macro when you want WordPerfect to perform that particular task.

We don't intend to go into great detail about the capabilities of the Macro feature in this section, but we do want to point out that, with a little imagination, you can use macros to take the drudgery out of text entry and formatting.

Increasing efficiency with macros

A Text-Entry Macro

Let's create a simple macro that types the word *stroke* every time you run the macro:

1. Click an insertion point at the end of the *Age:* line, after the colon.

2. Choose Record from the Macro menu. WordPerfect displays this dialog box:

Recording a macro

3. In the Filename text box, type *s* as the macro's name, and then type *stroke* in the Descriptive Name text box.

Naming macros	Pausing	Macro keyboard shortcuts
In WordPerfect, macro names can be up to eight characters. Each macro is stored in a file of its own, so the names you assign your macros must follow DOS file-naming conventions (see page 23). ◆	If you begin recording a macro and need to pause to carry out a task that you do not want to be part of the macro, you can choose Pause from the Macro menu. Choose Pause a second time to continue the macro where you left off. ◆	You can assign a keyboard shortcut to your macros instead of a name. Simply choose Record from the Macro menu as usual but instead of typing a name in the Filename text box, press Ctrl (or Ctrl-Shift) and a letter or number key. After recording the macro, you can run it by pressing the chosen key combination. ◆

4. Click the Record button to return to the Editing screen. The *Recording Macro* message appears in the bottom-left corner of your screen.

5. Type a space, and then type *stroke*. The word is displayed on the screen as you type, allowing you to make any corrections before you finish defining the macro.

Stopping the recorder →

6. Choose Stop from the Macro menu to end the macro definition. Behind the scenes, WordPerfect adds the extension WCM to the filename S, and saves the macro file in the C:\WPWIN\MACROS directory.

Now play back, or run, the macro:

1. Press Ctrl-Backspace to delete the word *stroke* from the Editing screen, and type the following:

   The incidence of

Running macros →

2. Next, choose Play from the Macro menu. WordPerfect displays this dialog box:

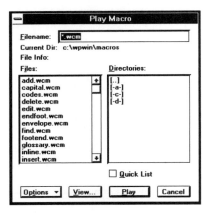

3. Select S.WCM in the Files list box, and click Play. WordPerfect inserts a space followed by the word *stroke* at the insertion point.

This might seem like a trivial example, but imagine the impact on your efficiency if the report included 20 instances of *acetylcholinesterase* or *Rebecca Brand vs. Midvalley Clinic*, instead of 20 instances of *stroke*.

Assigning a Macro to a Button   To increase your efficiency even more, you can assign the macro to a button on the Button Bar so that you can run the macro by simply clicking the button. Here's how:

1. Choose Button Bar Setup and Edit from the View menu, and in the dialog box, click Assign Macro To Button. WordPerfect displays this dialog box:

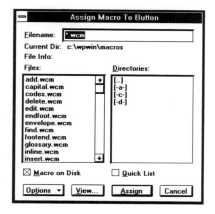

2. Select S.WCM, and click Assign. WordPerfect adds an S button at the end of the Button Bar (out of sight).
3. Click OK to close the Edit Button Bar dialog box.
4. Choose Button Bar Setup and Options from the View menu, click Left and Text Only, and then click OK. WordPerfect shifts the Button Bar to the left side of the screen, where all the buttons, including S, are visible.

Changing Button Bar positions

Now all you have to do to insert the word *stroke* anywhere in the report is to click the S button. Let's continue:

Clicking a button to run a macro

1. Type a space, and continue the paragraph as follows, clicking the S button when you want to insert the word *stroke*:

    increases dramatically with age. The chances of stroke *are very small in young individuals. A sharp increase in the risk of* stroke *occurs in the population beyond 50 years of age.*

    Press Enter once to add some space.
2. Next, enter the following paragraphs after the *Hypertension:*, *Smoking:*, and *Diabetes:* headings to get an idea of the time you can save. Press Enter once after

each paragraph, and be sure to save the document when you've completed the last paragraph.

Hypertension: *The risk of* stroke *increases, as does that of heart disease, in humans who have elevated blood pressure. It has now been demonstrated by clinical trials that control of blood pressure is a major factor in reducing the incidence of* stroke. *Furthermore, the sooner increased blood pressure is diagnosed and treated, the greater the reduction of* stroke *as well as heart attack.*

Smoking: *Smoking is a well established risk for* stroke. *The longer an individual has smoked and the more they have smoked, the higher the risk of* stroke *as well as heart attack. It is now known that cessation of smoking at any time, despite the duration of smoking, will significantly reduce the risk of coronary disease and heart attack. Whether the same is true for* stroke *has yet to be demonstrated, but in all likelihood the same will apply.*

Diabetes: *Diabetes and some other chronic illnesses are associated with an increase in the incidence of* stroke. *Diabetics who do not have the other risk factors listed above are less likely to suffer* stroke. *Whether strict control of diabetes itself (maintaining as normal a blood sugar level as possible) reduces the risk of* stroke *is unknown at this time, but long-range clinical studies are in progress.*

A Text-Formatting Macro

For our second example, we'll show you how to create a macro that underlines headings:

1. Position the insertion point just after the colon in the first level-three heading, *Age:*.
2. Choose Record from the Macro menu. Type *u* in the Filename text box, type *Underline* in the Descriptive Name text box, and click Record.
3. When the *Recording Macro* message appears, press Shift-Home to select the entire heading. (You cannot use the mouse to select text when you are recording a

macro.) Then choose Underline from the Font menu to underline the heading.

4. Choose Stop from the Macro menu to end the macro definition.

Now let's play back the macro:

1. Position the insertion point after the colon in *Hypertension:*.

2. Choose Play from the Macro menu, select U.WCM, and click Play. WordPerfect underlines the heading.

3. Repeat these steps for the five other level-three headings. The report now looks like this:

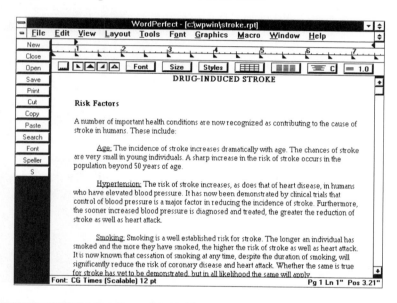

Reusable macros

When you create a macro, WordPerfect automatically saves the macro file with a WCM extension. The macro can then be used in any WordPerfect document. You can delete a macro file like any other WordPerfect file, by choosing Delete from File Manager's File menu. (See page 63 for more information about File Manager.) ◆

Macro directory

WordPerfect stores your macro files in a directory called C:\WPWIN\MACROS. You can change the directory by choosing Preferences and Location Of Files from the File menu, typing in the Macros\Keyboard\Button Bar text box the pathname of the directory where you want to store the files (for example, *c:\wpwin\text*), and clicking OK. ◆

Macro Button Bar

To create a Macro Button Bar to display buttons for macros so that they are readily available, choose Button Bar Setup and New from the View menu, assign the macros to a button bar, click Save As, and name the button bar. To display the button bar, choose Button Bar Setup and Select from the View menu, and double-click the Button Bar filename. ◆

4. Save the report by clicking the Save button on the Button Bar.

Creating Lists

In Chapter 2, you indented a numbered list in the example letter by selecting the numbered lines and choosing Paragraph and Indent from the Layout menu. Using this method worked because the list was very straightforward, and each item in the list was only one line long. In this section, we'll show you how to format lists with items more than one line long, and we'll show you how to use special characters to create professional-looking bulleted lists. In the process, you'll learn how to set custom tabs for those times when WordPerfect's default tabs don't meet your needs.

Numbered Lists

The example report contains a numbered list under the heading *Drugs That Damage Blood Vessels:*. Generally, you use numbered lists for step-by-step instructions or sequential processes. We'll use this example to demonstrate how to create a *hanging indent*, like the ones used for the instructions in this book. We'll create the hanging indents, use the Tab key to insert a fixed amount of space between each item's number (in this case, 1, 2, or 3) and its text, and see how to set custom tabs.

Start by typing the text of the numbered list:

1. Click an insertion point at the end of the *Drugs That Damage Blood Vessels:* heading, and type a space followed by this text (remember to click the S button on the Button Bar to insert the word *stroke*):

   A few drugs used for long periods of time can produce damage to blood vessels which weakens their walls and, in the case of arteries in the brain, may lead to stroke. *The evidence for the way in which these drugs produce this effect is not clear, but it is thought that it occurs in the following steps:*

2. Press Enter twice to create a blank line and start the first numbered item.

3. Press Tab to move over one tab, and then choose Paragraph and Hanging Indent from the Layout menu. Type *1.*, press Tab again, and type the following:

   With continual administration over long periods of time, the drug accumulates in the cells that line the artery.

Hanging indents

4. Press Enter twice to start the second numbered item.

5. Press Tab, and then press Ctrl-F7 (the keyboard shortcut for the Hanging Indent command). Type *2.*, press Tab again, and type

   As the drug accumulates, it gradually inhibits the cells' metabolic processes.

6. Press Enter twice. (Don't be alarmed if WordPerfect inserts a soft page break at this point; the position of the page break will change as you edit the text.)

Soft page breaks

7. Again press Tab and Ctrl-F7, type *3.*, press Tab again, and type

   Eventually, the cells of the artery die, leaving the vessel wall weakened and vulnerable.

8. Press Enter just once this time. The numbered list now looks like this:

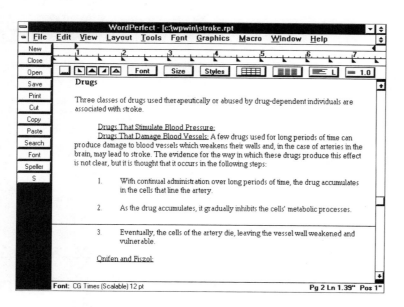

So far, so good. But notice that using the default tab settings produces a rather large space between the numbers and their corresponding text. Let's tighten up the spacing a bit by setting custom tabs at the beginning of the list. Follow these steps:

1. Click an insertion point just before the 1. in the numbered list.

Custom tabs

2. From the Layout menu, choose Line and Tab Set. WordPerfect displays this dialog box:

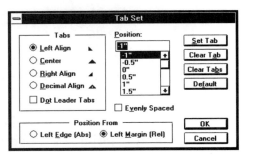

Clearing default tabs

3. Click Clear Tabs, and then click OK to delete the default tab settings.

4. Point to the Left Tab icon and drag a tab to the 1.5-inch mark on the Ruler. Then drag another tab to the 1.75-inch mark. Here's the result:

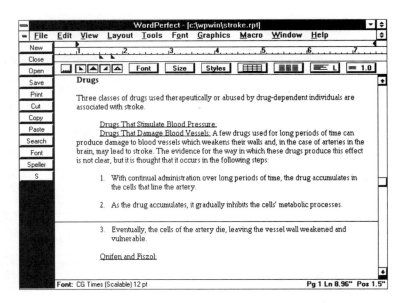

Now you must return the tabs to their default settings after the numbered list so that the custom tab settings don't affect the rest of the report.

1. Click an insertion point at the beginning of the *Qnifen and Fiszol* heading that follows the numbered list.
2. Choose Line and Tab Set from the Layout menu. In the dialog box, click Default, and then click OK.
3. Save the report by clicking the Save button on the Button Bar.

Restoring default tabs

Bulleted Lists

If you look back at the report shown at the beginning of the chapter, you'll see a bulleted list near the bottom of the first page. Generally, you use bullets for lists of items that are not sequential or hierarchical. In this example, we'll first use asterisks (*) as bullets; then we'll show you how to create real bullets.

As with the numbered list in the previous exercise, we'll set custom tabs. (If the items in your bulleted list are more than one line, you can create a hanging indent like the one in the numbered list.) Start by typing the text of the list:

1. Click an insertion point at the end of the *Drugs That Stimulate Blood Pressure:* heading, and type a space followed by this text:

   This first class of drugs includes adrenalin, amphetamines, and cocaine. Adrenalin is used therapeutically to raise blood pressure while both amphetamines and cocaine are commonly abused for their stimulatory effects. The principal actions of all these drugs are:

2. Press Enter twice to create a blank line and get ready for the first bulleted item.
3. To remove the default tabs, choose Line and Tab Set from the Layout menu, and click Clear Tabs in the Tab Set dialog box. Don't close the dialog box yet.
4. Next, select Left Edge in the Position From section. Then click an insertion point in the Position text box, type 1.5, and click Set Tab to set the first tab. Type 1.75 in the Position text box, click Set Tab again, and click OK to close the Tab Set dialog box.

Setting tabs in the Tab Set dialog box

Now for the bulleted items:

1. Press F7 (the keyboard shortcut for the Indent command), type *, press Tab to move over one tab, type *Increase blood pressure*, and then press Enter once to start the second bulleted item.

2. Press F7, type *, press Tab again, type *Increase heart rate*, and then press Enter once.

3. Press F7 again, type *, press Tab, type *Stimulate brain*, and press Enter once.

Now return the tab settings to their default settings:

1. Choose Line and Tab Set from the Layout menu, click the Default button, and then click OK. The bulleted list looks like this:

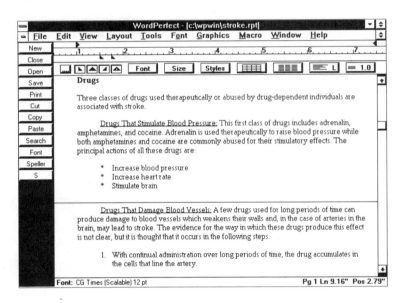

2. Save the report by clicking the Save button on the Button Bar.

Inserting Bullet Characters   Aside from the characters you see on your keyboard, WordPerfect can create a number of *special* characters, including math symbols, Greek characters, and letters with foreign accent marks. Some characters in the WordPerfect character sets don't appear in the Editing screen, but you can see them in the Print Preview screen. (Depending on your printer's capabilities, you might not be able to print all the available characters.)

Math symbols and Greek characters

A few of the characters available for use as bullets are •, °, and ○. For this example, we'll use a medium-sized filled bullet, like the one used in the report shown at the beginning of the chapter. Follow these steps:

1. Click an insertion point in front of the asterisk preceding the first bulleted item, and press Del to delete the asterisk.

2. To insert a medium-sized filled bullet, choose WP Characters from the Font menu. WordPerfect displays this dialog box:

Making bullets

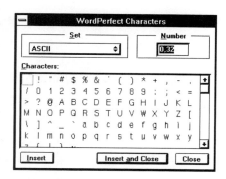

3. In the Number edit box, type *4,0.* (You specify the bullet by typing the character-set number—in this case 4—followed by a comma and the character number—in this case 0.) WordPerfect draws a box around the character you select so that you can see exactly which one will be inserted.

Character set numbers

4. Click Insert to insert the character. WordPerfect inserts a medium-sized filled bullet.

5. With the WordPerfect Characters dialog box still open, delete the asterisk in the second bulleted item, and click the dialog box's Insert button.

6. Repeat the previous step to replace the asterisk preceding the third bulleted item, clicking the Insert And Close button instead of the Insert button.

7. To see the character-set number you have inserted, choose Reveal Codes from the View menu, and move the cursor to the bullet character. Choose Reveal Codes again to return to the Editing screen.

8. Save the report by clicking the Save button.

Adding Footnotes

Some reports are more likely to have footnotes than others. If you use information from outside sources or want to steer readers toward data that backs up your arguments, you'll probably want to give credit or bibliographic information in footnotes, rather than cluttering up the body of the report.

In this section, we show you how to create the footnote that you can see on page two of the example report at the beginning of the chapter. This footnote occurs in a paragraph that we need to type below the *Qnifen and Fiszol:* heading.

1. Click an insertion point at the end of the *Qnifen and Fiszol:* heading, and press Enter twice to start a new paragraph.

2. Type the following, using the stroke macro where appropriate:

   Although both Qnifen and Fiszol appear to be equally effective in treating osteoporosis, they differ greatly in their chemical structures. While Qnifen contains one methyl group (CH3), Fiszol has none. This structural difference may explain why patients taking Qnifen have a higher incidence of stroke *than patients taking Fiszol. The following statement was recently published in the New World Journal of Medicine:*

3. If you want, italicize the name of the journal, and then press Enter twice to start a new line.

Double-indenting

4. From the Layout menu, choose Paragraph and Double Indent to indent the next paragraph—a quotation—from both the left and right margins. The insertion point moves to the first tab. Then press Ctrl-Shift-F7 (the keyboard shortcut for the Double Indent command) to move the insertion point over one more tab. Now type this:

   Fiszol would appear at this time to be a better choice than Qnifen in the treatment of osteoporosis, because of the early reports of fewer cases of stroke *associated with Fiszol.*

5. Check the results in the Print Preview screen, clicking 100% for a closer look, as shown here:

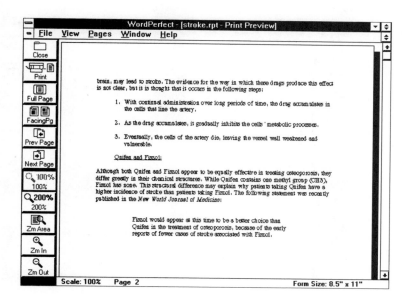

6. Close the Print Preview screen, and save the report by clicking the Save button.

Now we're ready to create the footnote:

1. Press Ctrl-End to be sure the insertion point is located after the period in the quotation.

2. From the Layout menu, choose Footnote and Create. A special Note Editing screen appears with the number of this footnote in the top-left corner and the type of note (Footnote or Endnote) in the title bar, as shown on the next page.

Subscript

To subscript a character, follow these steps: **1.** Select the character (for example, the 3 in CH3). **2.** Choose Subscript from the Font menu. ♦

Entering footnotes

You can type the text of the footnote in the Note Editing screen just as you would type text in the normal Editing screen, using such attributes as Bold, Italic, and Underline. You can also use any of WordPerfect's editing techniques, as well as the Speller, Thesaurus, and Reveal Codes. ♦

Setting off footnotes

By default, WordPerfect inserts a 2-inch line between a footnote and the text. Here's how to change the separator line: **1.** Choose Footnote and then Options from the Layout menu. **2.** Select No Line, 2-Inch Line, or Margin To Margin in the Separator section of the Footnote Options dialog box. **3.** Then click OK to return to the Editing screen. ♦

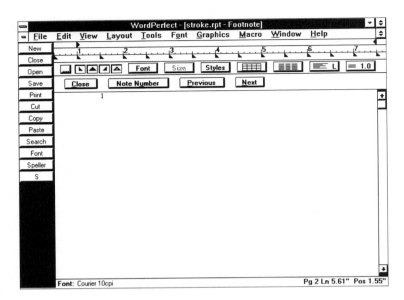

3. With the insertion point at the top of the Note Editing screen, click the Font button on the Button Bar, select Times, and click OK.

4. Type the following in the Note Editing screen:

    R. Urban, "Fiszol versus Qnifen and Stroke." New World Journal of Medicine, 217: 312-315, 1992.

5. Click Close to save the footnote and return to the Editing screen. WordPerfect has inserted the number 1 after the quotation.

Styles

If you often use the same combination of formatting for similar elements in your documents, you might want to consider using WordPerfect's Styles feature. The Styles feature let's you define a style, and then apply it to an element simply by selecting the style from the Styles list on the Ruler. For example, you might create a heading style that consists of 14-point Univers Italic, with center justification. Here's how you define this style in WordPerfect for Windows: **1.** Choose Styles from the Layout menu, and then click Create in the Styles dialog box. **2.** In the Style Properties dialog box, enter *heading* in the Name text box and an optional description in the Description text box. **3.** In the Type section, select Paired. **4.** Click OK to display the Style Editor window, which resembles a document window. The name you entered for the style is displayed in the title bar. In the Reveal Codes portion of the window (which is activated by default) is a Comment code that represents the text element to which you want to assign the style. **5.** Use the menus, Button Bar, and Ruler at the top of the window to create the style you want. For example, to create the heading style, click the Font button on the

6.   You can't see the footnote itself in the Editing screen, but you can see it if you choose Print Preview from the File menu to display the Print Preview screen. Then click Close to return to the Editing screen.

You can use this procedure to add footnotes anywhere in your document. For each footnote, WordPerfect inserts a Note code ([Footnote:#;[Note Num]*Text* ...], where # is the footnote reference number, and *Text* is the first few characters of the footnote text). If you insert a new footnote before an existing footnote, WordPerfect automatically renumbers the existing footnote. For example, if you add a footnote to page one of the report, WordPerfect changes the number of the footnote you just created to 2. You can delete a footnote by deleting the Note code in the Reveal Codes screen or by deleting the footnote reference number in the Editing screen. When you delete a footnote, WordPerfect automatically renumbers the remaining footnotes.

Deleting footnotes

Editing Footnotes

You can edit an existing footnote if you know its reference number. Follow the steps below to add formatting to the footnote you just created:

1.   From the Layout menu, choose Footnote and Edit. WordPerfect displays this dialog box:

Button Bar, and select 14-point Univers and Italic from the Font dialog box. Then select Center from the Justification list on the Ruler. **6.** When you are finished, click Close. The name of the style now appears in the Styles dialog box. **7.** Click Close to return to the Editing screen. Now all you have to do to apply the style is select the text you want to format and select the desired style from the Styles list on the Ruler. ♦

Paired vs. Open styles

A Paired style inserts a Style On and a Style Off code so that any formatting used in the style doesn't affect the text preceding or following the text element to which it's been applied. An Open style does not insert a Style On and a Style Off code and therefore affects the entire document. If you define an Open style with a format, such as Full justification,

your whole document will be full-justified unless another style somewhere else in the document changes the justification. Paired styles are useful for creating heading styles whereas Open styles are useful for creating any styles that include formatting, such as margins, and that you want to affect the entire document. ♦

2. Type *1*, and click OK.

3. When WordPerfect displays the footnote in the Note Editing screen, select *New World Journal of Medicine*. Then choose Italic from the Font menu to make the journal name italic.

4. Next, select the number 217, and choose Underline from the Font menu to add underlining.

5. Click anywhere in the screen to remove the highlighting, and click Close to save your changes and return to the Editing screen.

6. Save the report by clicking the Save button, and then check how the edited footnote looks in the Print Preview screen.

Footnote Placement

When you add a footnote to a document, WordPerfect places the footnote at the bottom of the page on which the reference number occurs and separates the footnote from the main text with a 2-inch line. If the footnote is too long to fit entirely on the page, WordPerfect tries to retain at least 1/2 inch of the footnote text on the same page as its reference number. If the footnote simply won't fit, WordPerfect breaks the page, moving both the text containing the reference number and the footnote to the next page.

Endnotes → You can tell WordPerfect to put your notes at the end of a document instead of at the foot of a page by choosing Endnote instead of Footnote from the Layout menu.

Creating Parallel Columns

Parallel columns, also called *side-by-side paragraphs*, are useful for creating documents such as inventory descriptions and presentation notes. The easiest way to understand this concept is to look at an example.

In the report shown at the beginning of the chapter, parallel columns are used in the middle of the second page to summarize the characteristics of Qnifen and Fiszol. You cannot use tabs or indents to create parallel columns; you must use WordPerfect's Columns feature. Start by writing a lead-in paragraph for the parallel-column format:

1. Click an insertion point at the end of the *Qnifen and Fiszol:* heading.
2. Type a space, and then type the following text, remembering to use the stroke macro:

   Both of these drugs are used to treat osteoporosis (softening of the bone). Both have also been associated with stroke*, but to varying degrees. A summary of the drugs is given below:*

3. Press Enter once to insert a blank line, and then press Down Arrow once to move the insertion point to the second blank line below the paragraph you just typed.

Now set up the columns, as follows:

1. From the Layout menu, choose Columns and then Define. WordPerfect displays this dialog box:

Setting up parallel columns

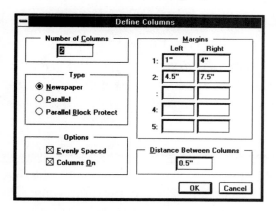

2. Click Parallel in the Type section, and in the Margins section, select the first default Left entry, and type *1.5* as the left margin of the first column. Then select the *second* default Right entry, and type *7.0* as the right margin of the second column.
3. Click OK. When you return to the Editing screen, notice that the status bar indicates an insertion point position of 1.5. As you can see, the left and right margins of the first column are 1.5 and 4.0 inches, and

the left and right margins of the second column are 4.5 and 7.0 inches.

4. Before you enter the text for the parallel columns, you need to insert a Column Off code ([Col Off]) after the Column On code ([Col On]). WordPerfect then knows that the rest of the report text is not part of the parallel column format. Without moving the insertion point, choose Columns and Columns Off from the Layout menu. WordPerfect inserts a Hard Page code and a Column Off code in your document.

Turning off parallel columns

You can now position the insertion point between the Column On and Off codes and type the text of the columns.

1. Choose Reveal Codes from the View menu, and place the cursor on the Hard Page code [HPg]. Choose Reveal Codes again to return to the Editing Screen, and then type the following text:

   Qnifen was the first drug developed for the treatment of osteoporosis. However, after prolonged use, it became associated with stroke.

Moving from column to column

2. Press Ctrl-Enter to move the cursor to the top of the second column, and type the following:

   Fiszol was recently approved for the treatment of osteoporosis. Because Fiszol has a different structure from Qnifen, current theory is that Fiszol will not have

---

Newspaper columns

In addition to using the Columns feature to create parallel columns, you can create newspaper columns that "snake" from one column to the next. So if you are responsible for creating the company newsletter, have no fear, WordPerfect's Columns feature is here! The easiest way to create this format is as follows: **1.** Point to the Columns button on the Ruler, and hold down the mouse button. **2.** Select 2, 3, 4, or 5 Columns. That's it! Your text is instantly reformatted from top to bottom and from left to right in the number of columns you specified. If you don't want a particular column to extend the length of the page, simply press Ctrl-Enter to end that column and move to the next one.

WordPerfect allows you to define up to 24 snaking columns, but you have to specify more than five columns through the menu. Here are the steps: **1.** Choose Columns and Define from the Layout menu. **2.** In the Define Columns dialog box, select the number of columns you want. **3.** Be sure Newspaper is selected in the Type section, and then set your margins. **4.** Click OK to return to the Editing screen. ♦

the same side effects. However, clinical trials have not yet corroborated this theory.

The parallel columns look like this:

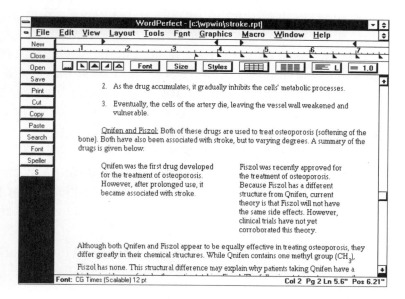

3. Save the report by clicking the Save button.

To start a new set of parallel paragraphs below this set, you would press Ctrl-Enter at the end of the paragraph in the second column. WordPerfect would then insert a blank line beneath the longest paragraph and move the insertion point to the beginning of the next line in the first column, ready for you to type a new set of parallel paragraphs.

If you decide to format existing text in parallel columns, position the insertion point where you want to start, and select Parallel as usual. Then position the insertion point in front of the text you want to move to the second column, press Ctrl-Enter, position the insertion point in front of the text you want to move back to the first column, press Ctrl-Enter, and so on.

Turning existing text into parallel columns

Adding Page Headers

Take a look at page two of the report shown at the beginning of the chapter. The page has a header at the top. A header is a line of text containing information, such as a report title, a date, or the name of your company, that you want to appear on all the pages of your document. The advantage of using a header is that you create it once and then leave it up to WordPerfect to place it at the top of the pages for you. You can have two different headers on a page, and you can specify on which pages they should appear.

Follow these steps to create a header for the report:

1. Be sure the insertion point is located on page one of the report. (WordPerfect's Auto Code Placement feature ensures that the Header code will be inserted at the top of your document—see page 51.)

2. From the Layout menu, choose Page and then Headers. WordPerfect displays this dialog box:

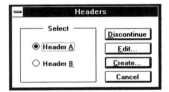

Headers that stand out

Adding attributes to the header, such as Small and Italic, will help it stand out from the rest of the text in the document. You can also draw lines to separate the header from the text (see page 69). ◆

Multiple headers

You can create two different headers for each page of your document by designating one as Header A and the other as Header B. You can place both of the headers on the same page, or you can place one header on even-numbered pages and one on odd-numbered pages. ◆

Footers

You can create footers, which appear at the bottom of the page, by using the procedures described for headers, except that you choose Page and Footers from the Layout menu instead of Headers. ◆

3. Click Header A in the Select section, and then click Create. WordPerfect displays a Header Editing screen, in which you enter the text of the header.

4. Type *Fox & Associates*. Then choose Line and Flush Right from the Layout menu, and type *Drug-Induced Stroke*. Here's how your screen looks now:

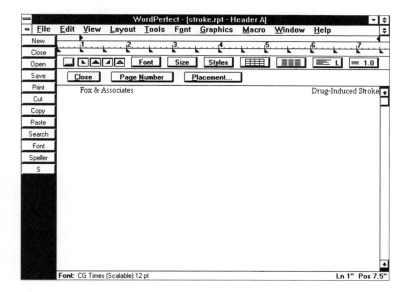

5. Click the Close button to save the header and return to the normal Editing screen.

Saving a header

6. To see the Header code [Header A:Every page;Fox & Associates[Flsh Rgt]Drug[-]Induced Stroke] at the beginning of the report, choose Reveal Codes from the View menu. When you're ready, choose Reveal Codes again to return to the Editing screen.

Editing an Existing Header

You can change a header by displaying it in the Header Editing screen and then editing it just as you would in the normal Editing screen. When you move to the Header Editing screen, WordPerfect searches backward and then forward, displaying the first header it finds. To edit a specific header, place the cursor on the desired Header code in the Reveal Codes screen before you move to the Header Editing screen.

For practice, edit the header you just created:

1. From the Layout menu, choose Page and Header, and then click Edit in the Headers dialog box. The Header Editing screen appears, displaying Header A.
2. To make the header smaller, select the entire header, and choose Size and then Small from the Font menu.
3. To make it italic, choose Italic from the Font menu.
4. Click the Close button to save the header and return to the Editing screen.

As with the footnote that you created earlier in the chapter, you cannot see the header in the Editing screen. You can, however, check it in the Print Preview screen:

1. Choose Print Preview from the File menu. Press the Next Page button to see the header on the second page.
2. Click the Close button on the Print Preview Button Bar to return to the Editing screen, and then save the report by clicking the Save button.

Suppressing Headers

You may have noticed in the Print Preview screen that the header on page one of the report is crowding the report title. To eliminate this problem, the first page of a document often does not have a header. Because headers often contain the same information as the document's title page, suppressing the header on this page also avoids redundancy.

Follow these steps to suppress Header A on page one of the example report:

1. Press Ctrl-Home to move the insertion point to the beginning of the report. (Suppressing a header affects only the page on which the insertion point is currently located.)
2. From the Layout menu, choose Page and then Suppress to display this dialog box:

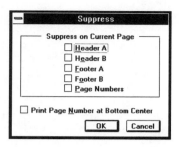

3. Click Header A, and then click OK.

4. Now save the report by clicking Save.

You can see the Suppress code [Suppress:HA] at the beginning of the report in the Reveal Codes screen, and you can see that the first-page header has been suppressed in the Print Preview screen.

Numbering Pages

WordPerfect's Page Numbering feature is easy to use and efficient. You can print numbers in one of eight different positions on the page and in one of three different numbering schemes—Arabic (1, 2, 3, 4), lowercase Roman (i, ii, iii, iv), or uppercase Roman (I, II, III, IV).

Numbering schemes

Follow these steps to number the pages of the report:

1. Press Ctrl-Home to move the insertion point to the top of the report.

2. From the Layout menu, choose Page and then Numbering. WordPerfect displays this dialog box:

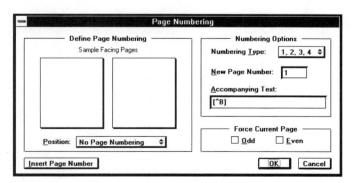

3. Click the arrows at the right end of the Numbering Type box to see the available number formats. Retain

the default 1, 2, 3, 4 option and the default New Page Number option of 1.

4. Click the arrows at the right end of the Position box to display the eight possible numbering positions, and select Bottom Center to print a page number at the bottom center of every page. The Sample Facing Pages graphics show how the page numbers will be positioned in the report.

5. Click OK to return to the Editing screen, and then click the Save button to save the report.

Positioning the numbers

WordPerfect has inserted the Page Numbering code [Pg Numbering:Bottom Center] at the beginning of the report. You can see this code in the Reveal Codes screen.

Printing the Report

At last you're ready to print the report. First let's take a look at it in the Print Preview screen, where we'll be able to see the page numbers, headers, and footnotes all in place:

1. Choose Print Preview from the File menu.

2. Click the 100% button on the Print Preview Button Bar, and scroll to the bottom of each page to see the page numbers, ending up on page two.

Suppressing page numbers

You can also use the Suppress feature to keep page numbers from being printed on selected pages. (Suppressing page numbers does not disrupt the page numbering in your document.) For example, you might want to suppress numbers on pages that have only graphics. ◆

Customizing pages numbers

You can tell WordPerfect to insert text along with the page number by following these steps: **1.** Choose Page and then Numbering from the Layout menu. **2.** In the Page Numbering dialog box, type the text you want in the Accompanying Text text box. You can include characters from the WordPerfect character sets (see page 97). For example, to insert the word *Page* before every page number, type the word *Page* followed by a space in the Accompanying Text text box. **3.** Click OK. The text-box entry must include a ^B code, which represents the actual page number. If you don't insert ^B, WordPerfect appends it to your entry. ◆

3. Click the Print button on the Print Preview Button Bar
    to display the Print dialog box.

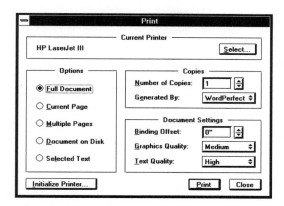

4. Click Current Page to print only the page on which the
    insertion point is currently located. WordPerfect prints
    page two of the report.

*Printing the
current page*

You can also select Multiple Pages to display the Multiple
Pages dialog box, where you can specify the range of pages
you want WordPerfect to print. For example, if your report
were four pages long, you would enter *2-3* in the Range text
box to print the second and third pages. (See the tip on page
67 for more details.)

*Printing a range
of pages*

Finally, save the report one more time, so that you can use
it in the next chapter where we discuss ways of dressing up
documents with graphics and tables.

Line numbering

You can use WordPerfect's
Line Numbering feature to
place a number beside every
line of text in a document.
(Footnotes and endnotes are
included in line numbering;
headers and footers are not.)
Line numbers are useful in
documents such as legal contracts, where particular lines
might need to be referenced.
   To turn on line numbering: **1.** Be sure the insertion
point is at the location where
you want line numbering to
begin. **2.** From the Layout
menu, choose Line and
Numbering. **3.** Select Con-
tinuous from the Line Numbering drop-down list box,
and then click OK. Although
the actual line numbers don't
appear in the normal Editing
screen, you can see them in
Print Preview and in the
printed document. ◆

Line-numbering options

If you select the Restart Each
Page option rather than Con-
tinuous in the Line Numbering drop-down list box, then
WordPerfect restarts the line
numbers on each page of the
document. You can also specify line-number position from
the left page edge, the starting number, whether to number all lines or skip some lines,
and whether to number blank
lines. ◆

5

Visual Aids

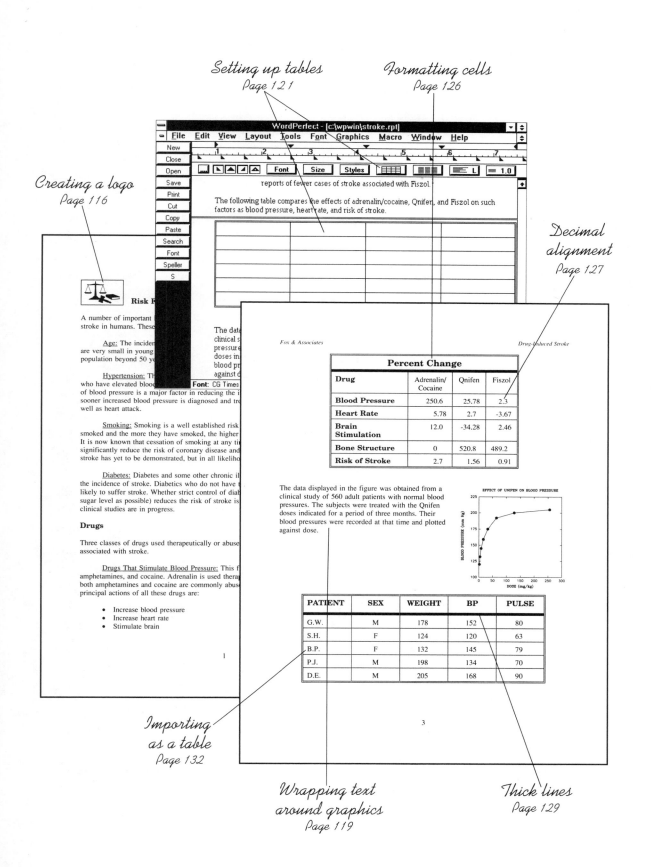

Setting up tables
Page 121

Formatting cells
Page 126

Creating a logo
Page 116

Decimal alignment
Page 127

Importing as a table
Page 132

Wrapping text around graphics
Page 119

Thick lines
Page 129

Successful computer applications have to be "friendly" toward their users, and in previous chapters, you have seen how easy WordPerfect for Windows is to learn and use. But these days, user-friendliness is not enough. Any application that aspires to best-seller status must also be friendly toward other applications. In this chapter, we'll show you how easily you can incorporate graphics and files that you've created in other applications into your Word-Perfect documents.

This chapter also covers how to create tables to present your facts and figures. And, if you've already set up your information in a spreadsheet program and don't relish the thought of having to recreate it in WordPerfect, you'll be pleased to learn that you can import spreadsheet data directly into your WordPerfect documents.

Importing WordPerfect's Graphics

In Chapter 3, you merged a letterhead with the letter you created in Chapter 2. The letterhead was a separate text file that, after the merge, became part of the letter file. In a similar way, you can merge separate graphics files into your Word-Perfect documents.

Ready-made graphics

The WordPerfect for Windows software package includes a number of ready-made graphics files that are suitable for many different types of documents. We'll use one of these files (LAW.WPG) to demonstrate how easy it is to import graphics with WordPerfect. To follow along, the graphics files, which have WPG extensions, must be stored in the C:\WPWIN\GRAPHICS directory on your hard disk. (You probably copied the graphics files when you installed the program. If you didn't, you should copy them now.) Then, with WordPerfect loaded and the report document from Chapter 4 displayed on your screen, follow these steps:

1. Press Ctrl-Home to move to the top of the report.
2. From the Graphics menu, choose Figure and then Retrieve. WordPerfect displays this dialog box:

3. In the Files list box, select *law.wpg*, and click View. WordPerfect displays the graphic you have selected so that you can be sure it's the one you want.

4. Click Retrieve. That's it! WordPerfect briefly displays the message *Please Wait*, and when you return to the Editing screen, this is what you see:

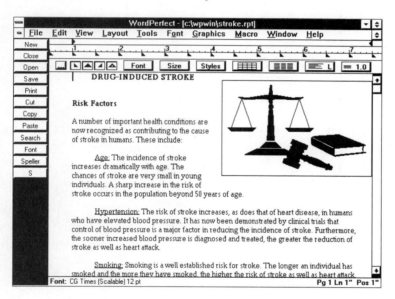

5. Display the Reveal Codes screen so that you can see the Figure Box code [Fig Box:1;law.wpg;], and then return to the Editing screen.

Changing the Graphic's Size

After you import the graphic, you can change its size and shape to suit the needs of your document. Let's turn the graphic into a small logo. Here's how:

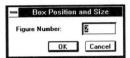

Creating a logo

1. From the Graphics menu, choose Figure, and then choose Position to display this dialog box:

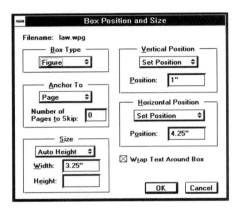

2. In the Figure Number text box, type *1* for Figure 1, and click OK. WordPerfect indicates that the graphic is selected by surrounding the graphic with black squares, called handles, and then displays this dialog box:

Justifying graphics

3. To left-justify the graphic, click the arrows in the Horizontal Position section, and select Margin, Left.
4. To change the width of the graphics frame, drag across the entry in the Width box in the Size section, and type *2* (for 2 inches). When the Auto Height option is selected, WordPerfect automatically adjusts the height of the graphics frame as you change the width, to maintain the original scale of the image.
5. Click OK to implement these changes.
6. Next, click the graphic to select it.
7. To decrease the graphic's size, position the insertion point on the handle in the bottom-right corner, and when the double-arrow pointer appears, drag it upward and to the left until the graphic fits neatly in the top-left corner of the first page of the report, like this:

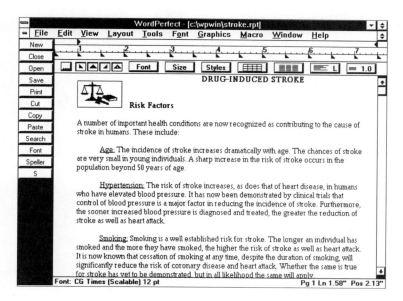

8. If your printer can handle graphics, print the first page of the report, and take a look at the new logo. Then save the report without changing its name by clicking the Save button on the Button Bar.

Importing Graphics Created with Other Applications

WordPerfect for Windows can use only graphics files that have been converted to a format called *WPG*. The conversion work is handled by WordPerfect's Graphics Conversion Program, which accepts files in a variety of graphics formats and converts them to WPG format. Before you can import a

The Figure Editor

You can access Word-Perfect's Figure Editor by choosing Figure and Edit from the Graphics menu, or by double-clicking the figure you want to edit. The Figure Editor comes with its own Button Bar, which you use to manipulate your figure's size and orientation. With the figure displayed in the Figure Editor screen, you can click the Move button and then use the mouse or Arrow keys to move the figure horizontally and vertically. (The Pos X and Y fields give you the figure's coordinates.) Use the Rotate button to rotate the figure. When you click Rotate, an X/Y axis appears. All you have to do is click and then drag the right end of the axis. Or you can point to a position on the figure and click the mouse to rotate the right end of the axis to that spot. To return the figure to its original orientation, simply click the Reset All button. To enlarge part of the figure, click Enlarge, and then click and drag a frame around the section you want to see, releasing the mouse button to display the enlargement. Click Reset Size to restore the figure to its original size. Click Mirror to create a mirror image of the figure and Outline to display the figure as a line drawing. ◆

graphic, you must first be sure that the graphic you want to import has been saved in one of the supported formats—EPS, PCX, and TIFF are some common examples.

In this section, we'll demonstrate how to import a graphic into the report. If you have a graphic available, you can follow along. We'll use this graphics file:

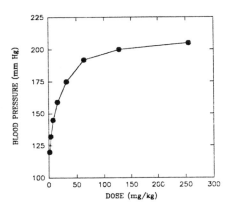

This chart, which is stored in a file called QNIFEN.PLT, was created with the SigmaPlot program. While in SigmaPlot, we saved the QNIFEN.PLT file in the HPGL (Hewlett-Packard Graphics Language) format, which is supported by Word-Perfect's Graphics Conversion Program. All we have to do is open the report and import the chart. The steps are simple:

1. With the report document still on your screen, move the insertion point to the desired location. (In this case, move to the end of the report by pressing Ctrl-End, and then press Ctrl-Enter to insert a page break so that the chart will appear on page three of the report.)

2. From the Graphics menu, choose Figure and Retrieve, select the graphics file in the Files list box or type the path and filename in the Filename edit box (we typed *c:\wpwin\qnifen.plt*), and click Retrieve. You will see the message *Please Wait* as WordPerfect converts and imports the graphic.

Converting graphics to WPG format

After importing the chart, you can make adjustments as follows:

1. Choose Figure and then Position from the Graphics menu, type *2* in the Figure Number text box, and click OK to display the Box Position And Size dialog box (see page 116) for the second graphic in the report.

2. In the Horizontal Position section, select Margin, Right.

3. In the Width and Height boxes in the Size section, decrease the width and height of the graphics frame so that you have room to add some text beside the chart. Because the Wrap Text Around Box option is selected, any text you add will wrap to the left of the chart.

   Wrapping text

4. In the Anchor To section, select Paragraph. The imported graphic will then be linked to any text you enter adjacent to the graphic and will move with the text if you edit the report, instead of remaining in a fixed position on the page.

   Linking text and graphics

5. Click OK to return to the Editing screen.

6. Now type the following text:

   The data displayed in the figure was obtained from a clinical study of 560 patients with normal blood pressures. The subjects were treated with the Qnifen doses indicated for a period of three months. Their blood pressures were recorded at that time and plotted against dose.

7. Next, move to the Reveal Codes screen and with the cursor on the Figure Box code, remove the border surrounding the graphic by choosing Figure and then Options from the Graphics menu. WordPerfect displays this dialog box:

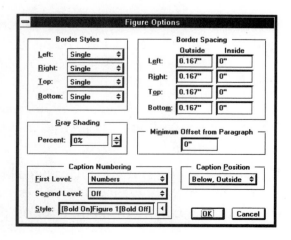

8. In the Border Styles section, select None from each of the Left, Right, Top, and Bottom lists. This is the result:

Creating Tables

Tables provide visual summaries of information and enable us to quickly grasp relationships that might be lost in narrative explanations. Why then are tables so difficult to create in most word-processing programs? Not so with WordPerfect for Windows. You specify the number of columns and rows and then leave it to WordPerfect to figure out the initial settings.

To demonstrate how easy the process is, we'll add a table to the example report. Start by adding a lead-in paragraph at the end of page two of the report:

1. Click an insertion point at the end of the quotation on page two, and press Enter twice to add a blank line and start a new line.

2. Type this text:

   The following table compares the effects of adrenalin/ cocaine, Qnifen, and Fiszol on such factors as blood pressure, heart rate, and risk of stroke.

3. Next, click an insertion point after the hard page break (check the placement in the Reveal Codes screen), and press Enter twice. The table will then begin on page

three of the report, above the chart and text we inserted earlier.

Now you can set up the table:

4. Press Up Arrow twice to move to the top of page three.

5. Point to the Tables button on the Ruler, and hold down the mouse button to display this grid:

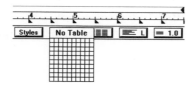

Specifying number of columns and rows

6. Drag the pointer across four columns and down six rows. WordPerfect shows the size of the selection above the grid. When you release the mouse button, this table appears in the document:

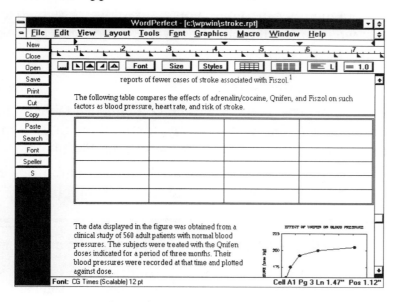

Notice that a double border surrounds the table, and single borders divide the columns and rows into cells. *Cell A1* is displayed at the beginning of the status line, letting you know that the insertion point is currently located in the cell at the intersection of the first column (column A) and the first row (row 1). Each cell in the table has a similar column/row address, allowing you to quickly determine the position of

Cell addresses

the insertion point by watching the status bar. You enter data in the Editing screen, as follows:

Inserting table entries

1. To enter the column headings, type *Percent Change* in cell A1, and press Tab to move to cell B1. Type *Adrenalin/Cocaine*, and press Tab to move to cell C1. Type *Fiszol*, and press Tab to move to cell D1. Finally, type *Qnifen*, and press Tab to move to cell A2.
2. Finish the table by typing the entries shown below, pressing Tab to move from cell to cell. (Pressing Shift-Tab moves the cursor to the previous cell, and you can also use the Arrow keys to move around.)

Blood Pressure	*250.6*	*2.3*	*25.78*
Heart Rate	*5.78*	*-3.67*	*2.7*
Brain Stimulation	*12.0*	*2.46*	*-34.28*
Bone Structure	*0*	*489.2*	*520.8*
Risk of Stroke	*2.7*	*0.91*	*1.56*

Looking over the table, you can see one or two changes that would make it more effective. We'll cover ways to edit tables next.

Rearranging the Table

You can rearrange the rows and columns in a table in much the same way that you rearrange text. Follow these steps to move the Qnifen column to the left of the Fiszol column:

Selecting columns

1. Point to cell D1, hold down the mouse button, and drag downward until the entire column is highlighted.

Printing tables

If your printer is unable to print graphics, it won't be able to print table lines either. If your printer is able to print graphics, and therefore is able to print table lines, don't be surprised if it prints documents containing tables and graphics more slowly than it does documents containing only regular text. ♦

Entering text in tables

When you add text to the table in the normal Editing screen, you can use most of WordPerfect's features, including appearance and size attributes, fonts, the Speller, and graphics. ♦

Deleting rows and columns

To delete one or more rows or columns, select them, and choose Tables and then Delete from the Layout menu. In the Delete Columns/Rows dialog box, select Columns or Rows, enter the number to be deleted, and click OK. If you don't select rows or columns first, WordPerfect deletes the rows or columns in which the insertion point is located. ♦

2. From the Edit menu, choose Cut, and then select Column. Click OK, and the Qnifen column disappears.

Moving columns

3. With cell C1 active, choose Paste from the Edit menu. WordPerfect inserts the Qnifen column to the left of the Fiszol column, as shown here:

Notice in the status bar that WordPerfect renumbered the columns so that the Qnifen column is now column C and the Fiszol column is column D. However, you are going to have to manually fix the double line between the Qnifen and Fiszol columns, as follows:

1. Drag down column C to select it, and then choose Tables and Lines from the Layout menu. WordPerfect displays the Table Lines dialog box.

Adjusting lines

Turning existing text into a table

If you want to turn a block of regular text that contains tabs into a real table, here's what you do: **1.** Select all the tabular text. **2.** Choose Tables, and then choose Create from the Layout menu. **3.** In the Convert Table dialog box, select Tabular Column, and click OK. ♦

Deleting tables

If you want to turn a table into regular tabular text, you can delete the table structure from around its contents. If you want to retain the table's structure but delete the table's current contents, you can clear the table cells. And you can also delete the table structure and its contents in one operation. Here's how: **1.** Select the entire table by dragging across all the cells. **2.** Press the Del key to display the Delete Table dialog box. **3.** Click the Contents button to delete the text entries, or click the Table Structure button to remove the table and convert the entries into tabular text. Leave the default Entire Table option selected to delete both the table's structure and its contents. **3.** Click OK to implement your selection. ♦

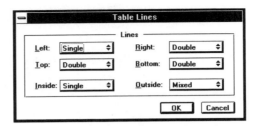

2.   You want to remove the line that has been drawn down the right side of the Qnifen column and over the left border of the Fiszol column, so click the arrows at the end of the Right box, and select None.

3.   Click OK to implement the change.

Inserting Rows

Suppose you want to use the *Percent Change* column heading as the table's title. The first step is to insert a new row at the top of the table. Follow these steps:

1.   Activate cell A1, and choose Tables and then Insert from the Layout menu to display this dialog box:

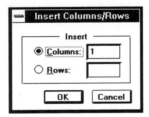

2.   Click Rows, and check that the number of rows to be inserted is 1.

3.   Click OK. WordPerfect displays the message *Please Wait* and then returns the table to the screen with a new row of four columns inserted at the insertion point. The new row has a double-line border above and below it, and the cells have all been renumbered so that the first cell in the new row is cell A1.

Joining Cells

Next, we must join the cells of the new row to create one large cell to accommodate the *Percent Change* heading. Joining cells is a simple two-step procedure.

1. Starting with cell A1, drag through cells A1 through D1 to select them.
2. From the Layout menu, choose Tables and then Join. The borders separating the columns in the first row disappear, creating one large cell.

Now finish the task by moving the column heading:

1. Drag through *Percent Change* in cell A2, and click the Cut button on the Button Bar. The selected text is removed from the cell and stored on the Clipboard.
2. Press Shift-Tab to move back to cell A1, and then click the Paste button to paste *Percent Change* into that cell.
3. Press Tab to move to cell A2, and type *Drug* as the new column heading.

Moving headings

Here's the result:

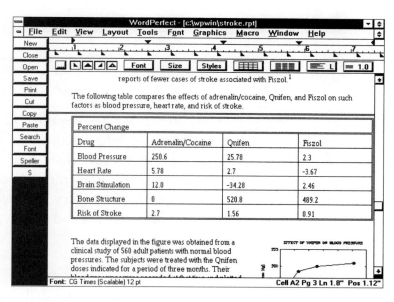

Changing Column Width

You can adjust column widths to suit your needs, by using menu options or moving the margin and column markers on the Ruler. Let's change the widths of some of the columns in the example table:

1. With the insertion point located anywhere in the table, drag the left margin marker (▶) to the 1.5-inch mark on the Ruler. WordPerfect adjusts the width of the columns to reflect the change.

2. Next, drag the first column marker (▼) to the 3.25-inch mark, the second column marker to the 4.25-inch mark, and the third column marker to the 5-inch mark.

3. Finally, drag the right margin marker (◄) to the 5.75-inch mark. Here's the result:

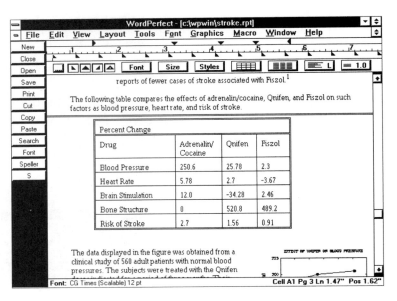

Multi Line setting

As you can see, the heading in cell B2 has wrapped to two lines. This is because WordPerfect's default Lines Per Row setting is Multi Line, meaning that WordPerfect will wrap an entry that is too long to fit in its cell to as many lines as necessary to display the entire entry. If the entry in only one cell in a row is multi-line, WordPerfect expands the whole row, as it did in our table.

Formatting Tables

Having made all the necessary structural changes to the table, let's add some formatting. We'll format the title and headings and align the number entries on the decimal point. Here's how:

Formatting cells

1. Activate cell A1, and choose Tables and Cell from the Layout menu. WordPerfect displays this dialog box:

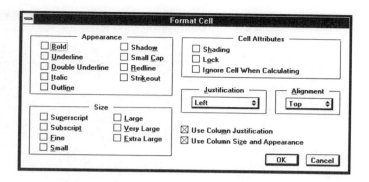

2. Select Bold to make the title bold and Large to make it larger.

3. Select Center from the Justification list in the Format Cell dialog box, and click OK.

4. To make the headings in the *Drug* column bold, click on the insertion point in A2, choose Tables and Column from the Layout menu, select Bold in the Format Column dialog box, and click OK.

    Formatting columns and rows

5. To center-justify the headings in cells B2 through D2, select the cells, and follow step 3 above.

6. To align the numbers in the *Adrenalin/Cocaine* column on the decimal point, select cells B3 through B7, choose Tables and Column from the Layout menu, select Decimal Align from the Justification list, and click OK.

    Decimal-alignment

7. Repeat the previous step to decimal-align the numbers in the *Qnifen* and *Fiszol* columns. The table now looks like the one on the next page.

Changing row height

You can set the row height to accommodate one line or multiple lines of text. With a single-line setting, text does not wrap within the cell, and pressing Enter moves the cursor to the next cell. With a multi-line setting, text does wrap, and pressing Enter moves the cursor to the next line within the cell. Here's how to change the Lines Per Row setting: **1.** With one of the cells of the row active, choose Tables and then Row from the Layout menu. **2.** In the Format Row dialog box, select Single Line, and click OK. WordPerfect then reformats the row.

You can also select fixed or automatic row height. With a fixed setting, you enter the height for each row. With an automatic setting, WordPerfect adjusts the height based on the size of the text within the row. ♦

Caution: Hidden text

WordPerfect won't print hidden text, so you must be very careful when adjusting the width of columns if the Lines Per Row option is set to Single Line. If you make a column so narrow that you truncate entries, you may not notice the problem until after you print and proofread the table. ♦

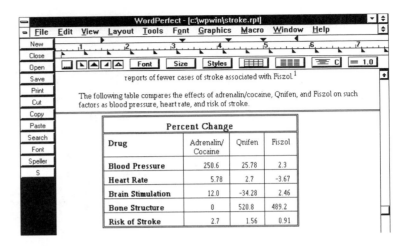

Changing Gridlines

Before we wrap up this section, let's add a final touch to the table by changing the line below the title:

1. Select cells A2 through D2, and choose Tables and Lines from the Layout menu to display this dialog box:

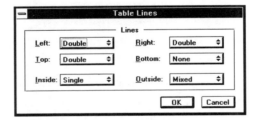

Table Button Bar

You can use WordPerfect's Table Button Bar to format your tables instead of having to choose Table commands from the Layout menu. Here's how to display the Tables Button Bar: **1.** Choose Button Bar Setup, and then choose Select from the View menu. **2.** Highlight the TABLES.WWB file in the Files list box, and click Select. WordPerfect then loads the Table Button Bar in place of whichever Button Bar you were previously working with.

To activate the buttons on the Table Button Bar, be sure your insertion point is located within a table. You can click the buttons to access the same dialog boxes you access with the Tables command.

You can add commands to the Table Button Bar and change its location and appearance using the same techniques as those you used with the WordPerfect for Windows default Button Bar in Chapter 1 (see page 14). ◆

2. In the Top box, select Thick, and click OK. The result is this thick, shaded line below cell A1:

Thick lines

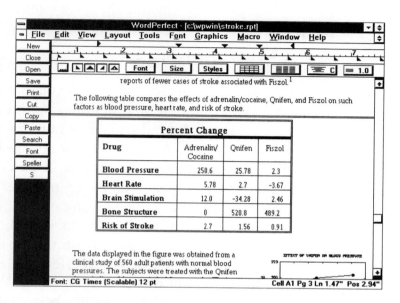

Centering the Table

With WordPerfect, you don't have to worry about adjusting margins to center the table between them. A couple of selections do the trick:

1. From the Layout menu, choose Tables and Options. WordPerfect displays this dialog box:

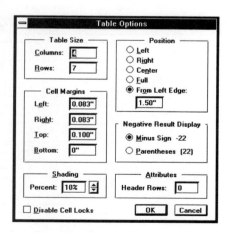

2. In the Position section, select Center, and click OK. The table is now centered between the left and right margins.

3. To see how the table looks on the page, display it in Print Preview.

4. Now save the report by clicking the Save button.

Importing Spreadsheets

Although WordPerfect's Table feature allows you to create impressive tables and do some mathematics with ease, it doesn't calculate complex formulas and functions the way a spreadsheet program does. And although a spreadsheet program is great for performing calculations, it lacks the word-processing capabilities you need to put together dynamic reports. Suppose you have gone to a lot of trouble to create a spreadsheet and you now want to include the spreadsheet's data in a report. It would be frustrating to have to rekey all that information into a WordPerfect table for presentation. Fortunately, you don't have to. With Word-Perfect for Windows, you can combine the best of both worlds—the numeric know-how of a spreadsheet program with the word-processing proficiency of WordPerfect.

To demonstrate, we'll pull this spreadsheet, which was created with Lotus 1-2-3, into the report:

PATIENT	SEX	WEIGHT	BP	PULSE	EEG	BONE/DEN
G.W.	M	178	152	80	4	23.5
S.H.	F	124	120	63	8	16.3
B.P.	F	132	145	79	9	12.7
P.J.	M	198	134	70	8	31.7
D.E.	M	205	168	90	7	30.9
C.E.	M	212	136	72	5	24.9
W.D.	F	156	127	65	5	17.9
T.W.	F	127	140	85	3	14.8
L.D.	F	117	128	69	7	20.7
G.A.	F	167	137	85	8	10.7
J.K.	M	179	148	74	5	22.7
A.M.	M	158	143	81	4	32.9

You can follow these steps with your own spreadsheet file:

1. Press Ctrl-End to move to the end of the report. Press Enter several times to insert blank lines and move the insertion point below the chart.

2. Choose Spreadsheet and Import from the Tools menu. WordPerfect displays this dialog box:

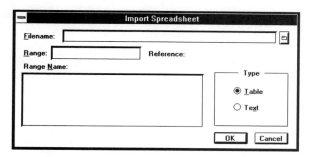

3. In the Filename text box, type the full path and filename of the spreadsheet to be imported (we typed *c:\wpwin\qnifen.wk1*).

4. If you don't want to import the entire spreadsheet, click the Range text box. Drag through the *<Spreadsheet>* entry, and type the range of cells you want to import, separating the first cell from the last cell in the range by a colon, one period, or two periods (depending on the range-addressing conventions of the program with which you created the spreadsheet). If you're unsure how to make this entry, check the Range Name list box.

Importing a range

Supported spreadsheet formats

Currently, files from the spreadsheet programs listed below can be imported into WordPerfect for Windows documents:

PlanPerfect
Lotus 1-2-3
Excel 3.0
Quattro and Quattro Pro ♦

Linking spreadsheets

You can use WordPerfect's Spreadsheet Link feature to create a dynamic link between a spreadsheet file and a WordPerfect document. To create a spreadsheet link: **1.** Choose Spreadsheet and Create Link from the Tools menu. **2.** Enter the spreadsheet's filename in the Create Spreadsheet Link dialog box. **3.** Enter a range in the Range text box, select

Table or Text, and click OK. WordPerfect inserts [Link] and [Link End] codes at the beginning and end of the spreadsheet in your Word-Perfect document. (These codes do not print; they merely tell you where the spreadsheet link begins and ends.) Now if you make changes to the spreadsheet file and then open the document, WordPerfect updates the document's version of the spreadsheet to reflect your changes. ♦

Importing as a table

5. To import the spreadsheet file as a WordPerfect table, accept the default setting of Table in the Type section, and click OK. WordPerfect displays the message *Importing Spreadsheet* and returns you to the Editing screen, where the spreadsheet file has been imported as a table at the insertion point:

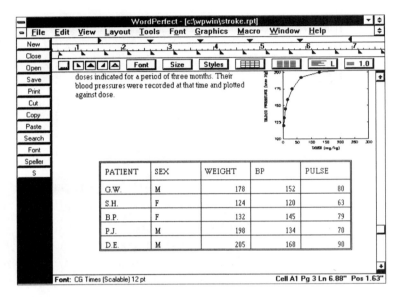

You can edit the table in the Editing screen using the techniques described earlier. On the facing page is the last page of the report after we made a few adjustments to the demonstration spreadsheet data.

By itself, WordPerfect can create some pretty fancy documents. Add a few graphics and a spreadsheet, and you've got documents with real distinction! WordPerfect's ability to import graphics and spreadsheets allows you to tap into valuable outside resources. So be adventurous, and let WordPerfect help you generate a report that will make your colleagues sit up and take notice.

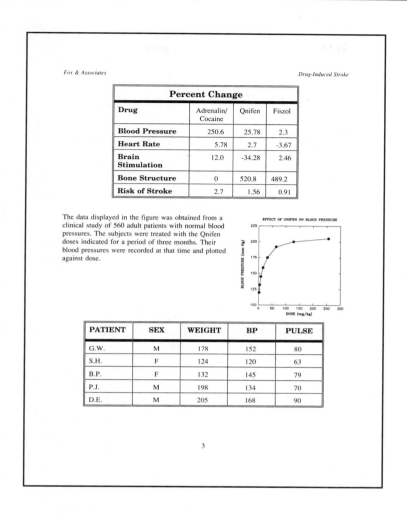

That's it for the report. Let's move on to Chapter 6, where we take a look at WordPerfect's Print Merge feature.

6

Time-Saving Form Documents

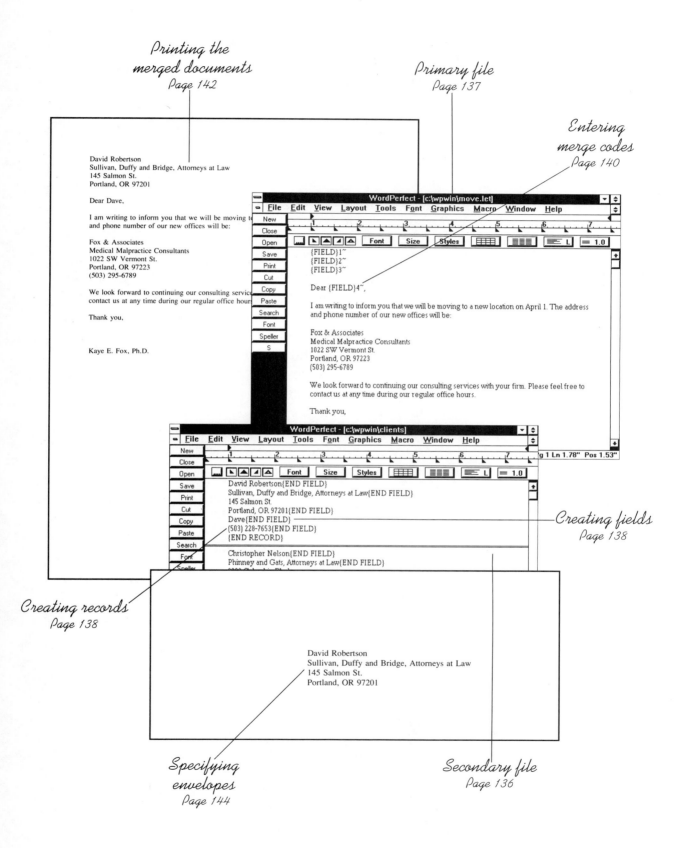

Printing the merged documents
Page 142

Primary file
Page 137

Entering merge codes
Page 140

Creating fields
Page 138

Creating records
Page 138

Specifying envelopes
Page 144

Secondary file
Page 136

If you need to send the same letter to half a dozen of your clients, you can create a template letter and quickly fill in the name, address, and salutation for each client. But what if you need to send the letter to a hundred clients? And what if you communicate regularly with the same set of clients? Isn't there a way to save having to type those names and addresses over and over again?

The time-saver you're looking for is WordPerfect's Merge feature. You can use Merge to create "personalized" letters and envelopes for mass mailings, as well as a whole host of other documents, such as phone lists, invoices, memos, and contracts. To use the Merge feature properly, you need to be familiar with some jargon, so we'll start with a few definitions, using a form letter as an example. To create a form letter, you need to create a primary file and a secondary file. Let's talk about the secondary file first.

Secondary file →

The secondary file contains the information that changes from letter to letter, such as the names and addresses of the recipients. Collectively, the information that will be merged into one letter—in this case, a name, company name, address, and salutation—is referred to as a record, and each item within one record is referred to as a field. To understand this relationship, take a look at this secondary file:

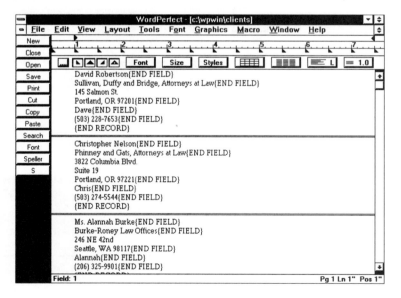

The records are separated by {END RECORD} codes, followed by hard page breaks. The fields within each record are separated by {END FIELD} codes followed by hard returns.

You can include as many records as you want (or as many as disk space permits) in a secondary file, and you can include an unlimited number of fields in each record. However, every record must contain the same number of fields, and every field must either contain the same type of information or be empty. For example, field 5 of every record in the example contains a phone number. If you have a record with no phone number, field 5 of that record remains empty but still ends with an {END FIELD} code and a hard return.

The primary file contains the information that does not change from letter to letter—the text of the letter. This file also controls the merging process by means of codes that you insert as placeholders for the information that does change from letter to letter. Here's an example:

Primary file

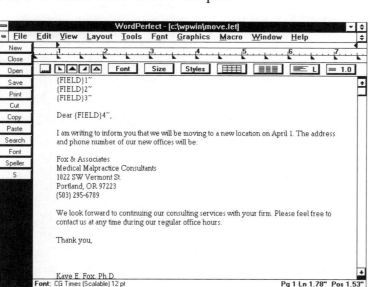

The {FIELD}1~ merge code is a placeholder for the information contained in field 1 in the records of the secondary file. The tilde (~) tells WordPerfect that the number 1 is part of the code and not part of the text of the letter.

Creating a Form Letter

Let's create the example primary and secondary files so that you can see how merging works. Because you will probably use the same secondary file with more than one primary file, you'll usually start by creating the secondary file, which in this case is a "database" of clients' names and addresses.

Creating the Secondary File

Each record in the secondary file we're going to create contains five fields: names in field 1, company names in field 2, addresses in field 3, salutation names in field 4, and phone numbers in field 5. Fields do not have to contain the same number of characters or even the same number of lines. For example, field 3 in the second record might contain an address that is three lines long, whereas field 3 in the third record might contain an address that is only two lines long.

Load WordPerfect, and starting with a clear screen, follow these steps to create the secondary file, using the suggested names and addresses or some of your own:

Creating fields

1. In a clear Editing screen, type *David Robertson*, and choose Merge and End Field from the Tools menu to insert an {END FIELD} code and a hard return at the end of the line. You've just created your first field.

2. On the second line, type *Sullivan, Duffy and Bridge, Attorneys at Law*, and press Alt-Enter (the keyboard shortcut for the End Field command). WordPerfect inserts an {END FIELD} code and a hard return.

3. On the third and fourth lines, type the following, pressing Enter after the third line and Alt-Enter after the fourth line:

    145 Salmon St.
    Portland, OR 97201

4. On the fifth line, type *Dave*, and press Alt-Enter.

5. On the sixth line, type *(503) 228-7653*, and press Alt-Enter.

Creating records

6. To end the record, choose Merge and End Record from the Tools menu. WordPerfect inserts an {END RECORD} code and a hard page break at the cursor. Here's what your first record looks like:

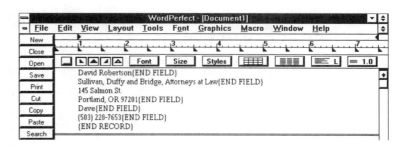

Now we can enter a couple of other records. Follow the preceding steps to enter the following information. Press Alt-Enter after each field, and press Alt-Shift-Enter (the keyboard shortcut for the End Record command) after each record. (Refer to the secondary file shown on page 136 to see where to press Enter and where to press Alt-Enter.)

Christopher Nelson
Phinney and Gats, Attorneys at Law
3822 Columbia Blvd.
Suite 19
Portland, OR 97221
Chris
(503) 274-5544

Ms. Alannah Burke
Burke-Roney Law Offices
246 NE 42nd
Seattle, WA 98117
Alannah
(206) 325-9901

Click the Close button on the Button Bar, and save the file with the name *clients* before WordPerfect clears the screen.

Creating the Primary File

Now we're ready to create a primary file that makes use of the secondary file's name and address database. Be sure the Editing screen is clear, and then follow these steps:

1. Press Enter twice, and type the following:

    I am writing to inform you that we will be moving to a new location on April 1. The address and phone number of our new offices will be:

    Fox & Associates
    Medical Malpractice Consultants
    1022 SW Vermont St.
    Portland, OR 97223
    (503) 295-6789

We look forward to continuing our consulting services with your firm. Please feel free to contact us at any time during our regular office hours.

Thank you,

Kaye E. Fox, Ph.D.

2. Press Ctrl-Home to move the insertion point to the beginning of the letter, where you are going to insert the first placeholder merge code.

Entering merge codes

3. From the Tools menu, choose Merge and Field. Word-Perfect displays this dialog box:

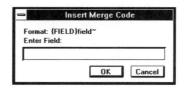

4. In the Enter Field text box, type *1*, and then click OK. WordPerfect inserts a {FIELD}1~ merge code.
5. Press Enter to start a new line, choose Merge and Field from the Tools menu, type *2* in the Enter Field text box, and click OK to insert a {FIELD}2~ merge code.
6. Repeat the previous step, typing *3* in the Enter Field text box to insert a {FIELD}3~ merge code.
7. Press Enter twice below the {FIELD}3~ merge code, and then type *Dear* followed by a space.
8. Without moving the insertion point, choose Merge and Field from the Tools menu, type *4*, and click OK to insert a {FIELD}4~ merge code after the word *Dear.*
9. Finally, type a comma after the {FIELD}4~ code. Your primary file now looks like the one on page 137.
10. Click Close, and save the primary file with the name *move.let* before WordPerfect clears the screen.

Merging and Printing the Files

This is the moment of truth. If you have inserted the codes correctly, merging the primary and secondary files will be a piece of cake. Just follow these steps:

1. With a clear Editing screen, choose Merge from the Tools menu, and then choose Merge from the cascading menu to display this dialog box:

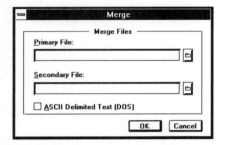

2. Type *move.let* in the Primary File text box and *clients* in the Secondary File text box, and click OK.

As WordPerfect merges the two files, it displays the message *Merging*. When the merging process is complete, you return to the Editing screen. You can then view and print the merged letters. Here's how:

1. Press Ctrl-Home to move the insertion point to the top of the first letter.

Viewing merged documents

Adding the current date

You can add the current date to your form letters by inserting a {DATE} code in the primary file. Follow these steps: **1.** Load the primary file. **2.** With the insertion point at the top of the document, press Enter three times to add space, and then press Ctrl-Home to return the insertion point to the top of the document. **3.** From the Tools menu, choose Merge and then Merge Codes. **4.** Press the Down Arrow key to move the highlight to the {DATE} merge code, click Insert to insert the code in the primary file, and then click Close. Now every time you merge the primary file, WordPerfect inserts the current date at the top of each document. ◆

Canceling printing

While WordPerfect is sending a print job to the Windows Print Manager, you can cancel the printing by clicking the Cancel Print Job button in the Current Print Job dialog box. After the file has gone to Print Manager, you must use Print Manager to cancel the print job. ◆

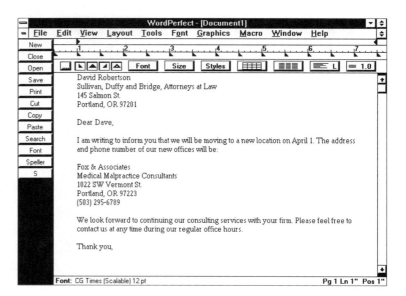

2. Press Alt-PgDn to move to the top of the second letter, and then press Alt-PgDn to move to the third letter. As you can see, WordPerfect replaced the merge codes in the primary file with the names and addresses from the secondary file to create a "personalized" letter for each record.

3. Click the Save button on the Button Bar, and save the document containing the letters as *move.mrg*.

4. Click the Print button, check that Full Document is selected, and click Print to print the letters. Because the letters are separated by hard page breaks, they print on separate pages.

5. Click the Close button to clear the screen.

Printing the merged documents

Editing the Primary File

You can use a field more than once in a primary file. For example, you can delete the words *your firm* from the last paragraph of MOVE.LET and insert a {FIELD}2~ merge code by choosing Merge and Field from the Tools menu, typing 2, and clicking OK. Here's the result:

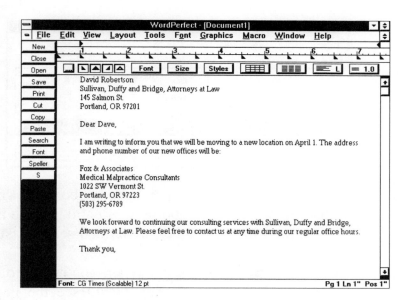

Printing Envelopes

We mentioned earlier that you will often use a secondary file with more than one primary file. If you use a name and address secondary file to create form letters, you will probably want to use that same secondary file to print envelopes. To print envelopes, you must create a primary file that defines the size of the envelope and contains the merge-code placeholders for the names and addresses.

If your printer does not have an envelope feed or cannot produce landscape fonts (which print perpendicular to the inserted edge of the envelope), you might not be able to print envelopes. However, if you follow along, you can check the Print Preview screen to see what the envelopes look like.

Setting the Paper Type

To print addresses on standard business envelopes (9 1/2 by 4 inches), start by selecting the paper type:

1. Be sure your screen is clear, and then choose Document and Initial Codes from the Layout menu. WordPerfect displays the Document Initial Codes screen.
2. From the Layout menu, choose Page and Paper Size to display the Paper Size dialog box:

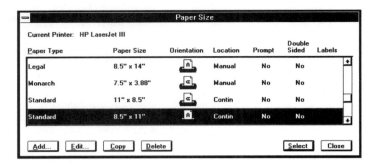

Specifying envelopes

3. Scroll to the top of the Paper Type list box, and click the Envelope 9.5" x 4" option to select it. Notice that the selection includes other predefined settings, such as Orientation.

4. Now click the Select button. When you return to the Document Initial Codes screen, you see the Paper Size/Type code [Paper Sz/Typ:9.5" x 4",Envelope].

Positioning the Address

Next, you need to set margins to position the address in the center of the envelope. Here's how:

1. With the Document Initial Codes screen displayed, choose Margins from the Layout menu to display this dialog box:

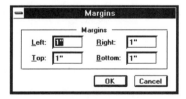

2. To print the names and addresses 4 inches from the left margin, type *4* in the Left text box and *0* in the Right text box. (See the tip on the next page.)

3. Type *2* in the Top text box so that the address prints 2 inches from the top of the envelope.

4. Type *0* in the Bottom text box (again, see the tip on the next page), and then click OK.

5. Click Close to close the Document Initial Codes screen and return to the Editing screen.

Inserting the Merge Codes

Now you're ready to insert merge codes into the primary file so that you can merge it with the existing secondary file:

1. From the Tools menu, choose Merge and then Field. In the Edit Field text box, type *1*, click OK to insert a {FIELD}1~ code, and press Enter to start a new line.
2. Repeat the previous step twice to insert a {FIELD}2~ code and a {FIELD}3~ code into the primary file.
3. Click the Close button on the Button Bar, and save the document with the name *envelope* before WordPerfect clears the screen.

Merging and Printing the Files

Now to test the accuracy of the settings and codes. Merge the primary and secondary files by following these steps:

1. Choose Merge and then Merge from the Tools menu, type *envelope* as the primary file and *clients* as the secondary file, and click OK.
2. Press Ctrl-Home to move the insertion point to the first "envelope." The other two are visible on your screen, but the hard page breaks ensure that they will print on separate envelopes.
3. Choose Print Preview from the File menu, and click Full Page to see how the first envelope will look when it's printed. Then click Close to return to the Editing screen.

Viewing the envelopes

No zeros please

Some laser printers will not allow you to specify settings of 0 inches for your margins. If your printer falls into this category, WordPerfect will probably prompt you to enter a minimum margin setting in steps 2 and 4 of the example above. Simply accept Word-Perfect's minimum allowable margin setting, and click OK. ◆

Creating phone lists

You could also use the information from a secondary file, like the one on page 136 to generate a phone list. All you have to do is create a primary file with a field code for the name field used in the secondary file. Then set a tab around the 3-inch or 4-inch position, and insert a field code for the phone number field used in the secondary file. Finally, press Enter to move the insertion point just below the first field code, and choose Merge and Page Off from the Tools menu to insert a {PAGE OFF} code, which turns off the hard page breaks that WordPerfect originally inserted in the secondary file. Now, save the new primary file, and perform the merge to create the phone list. ◆

4. Click the Save button, and save the document with the filename *envelope.mrg*.

5. Click the Print button to print the envelopes.

We printed the envelope shown below with a Hewlett-Packard LaserJet III printer.

David Robertson
Sullivan, Duffy and Bridge, Attorneys at Law
145 Salmon St.
Portland, OR 97201

Index

100% button 54
200% button 54

A

adding
    buttons to Button Bar 14
    fonts to Ruler 17
addresses of cells 121
adjusting lines in tables 124
aligning text 20
alignment
    changing 20
    decimal 127
anchoring graphics to text 119
applying attributes (formats)
    12
arranging windows 28, 73
assigning macros to buttons
    89
attributes
    and base font 46
    applying 12
    Bold 60, 68, 127
    deleting 11
    Italic 60, 68, 102, 108
    Redline 12
    Small 108
    Strikeout 12
    Underlining 102
Auto Code Placement 51

B

backing out of menus 11
backing up 24
    Original Backup option 24
    Timed Backup option 25
base font
    selecting 46–47
Bitstream fonts 47
BK! extension 24
BK1 extension 25
BK2 extension 25
Bold attribute 60, 68, 127
Bold command 11, 68
Bold Off code 22
Bold On code 22
borders, removing from
    graphics 119

bullet characters 96
bulleted lists 95
Button Bar
    changing position 14
    customizing 14, 15
    default 13
    displaying 10, 13
    editing 14
    Equation Editor 15
    Figure Editor 15
    giving instructions with
        13, 15
    loading different 15
    moving buttons on 15
    predefined 15
    Secondary 15
    Table 15
Button Bar command 10
Button Bar Setup, Edit
    command 14
Button Bar Setup, Options
    command 14
Button Bar Setup, Select
    command 91
buttons
    Cancel 9
    command 9
    Maximize 29
buttons (Button Bar) 13
    adding 14
    assigning macros to 89
    changing position of 14
    Close 15, 34, 63, 67
    Copy 38, 72
    Cut 37
    Font 17–18, 49, 59–60, 68
    moving 15
    Open 26, 65
    Paste 37, 39, 73
    Print 61, 67, 71, 74
    Save 23, 25, 34, 50, 61, 72
    Search 41–42
    Speller 44
    text-only 14
buttons (Print Preview
    Button Bar)
    100% 54
    200% 54
    Full Page 54
    Print 54
    Zm In 54
    Zm Out 54

buttons (Ruler)
    Columns 17
    Font 17
    Justification 20
    Size 19
    Spacing 51
    Tables 121

C

Cancel button 9
canceling
    commands 11
    printing 141
capitalization, detecting
    inappropriate 43, 45
capitalizing text 3
cascading menus 9
cells
    addresses of 121
    joining 124
    in tables 121
center justification 20–21, 58
centering
    tables 129
    text 58, 69, 127
    vertically 52
changing
    alignment 20
    column width 125
    date code format 63
    default formatting 48
    directories 27
    font 17–18
    graphic size 115
    graphic width 116, 119
    gridlines 128
    initial codes 48
    justification 20
    line spacing 50
    line thickness 69
    margins 49
    numbering style 83
    outline levels 81
    position of Button Bar 14
    row height 127
    size 19, 60–61
characters
    bullet 96
    kerning 61
    selecting 60
    spacing evenly 61
    special 96
checking spelling 43

Acknowledgments

Many thanks to Paul Eddington at WordPerfect Corporation.

About Online Press

Founded in 1986, Online Press is a group of publishing professionals working to make the presentation and access of information manageable, efficient, accurate, and economical. In 1991 we began publishing our popular *Quick Course* computer-book series, offering streamlined instruction for today's busy professional. At Online Press, it is our goal to help computer users quickly learn what they need to know about today's most popular software programs to get their work done efficiently.

Cover design and photography by Tom Draper Design
Interior text design by Salley Oberlin, Joyce Cox, and Kjell Swedin
Graphics by Polly Urban
Layout by Joyce Cox and Bill Teel
Typeset by Seattle Imagesetting
Printed by Viking Press Inc.
Otabind® cover by Muscle Bound Bindery

Text composition by Online Press in Times Roman, with display type in Helvetica Narrow Bold, using Ventura Publisher and the Linotronic 300 laser imagesetter.

Other *Quick Course* Books

Don't miss the other titles in our *Quick Course* series! Quality books at the unbeatable price of $12.95.

Available now...

A Quick Course in Windows
A Quick Course in DOS 5
A Quick Course in WordPerfect 5.1
A Quick Course in Excel for Windows

Coming soon...

A Quick Course in Word for Windows   (January 1992)
A Quick Course in Lotus 1-2-3 for Windows   (Early 1992)
A Quick Course in Quattro Pro for Windows   (Spring 1992)
A Quick Course in Paradox for Windows   (Spring 1992)

Plus more to come...

For our latest catalog, call (800) 854-3344 or write to us at:
Online Press Inc., 14320 NE 21st Street, Suite 18, Bellevue, WA 98007